LEEDS

in the age of the tram

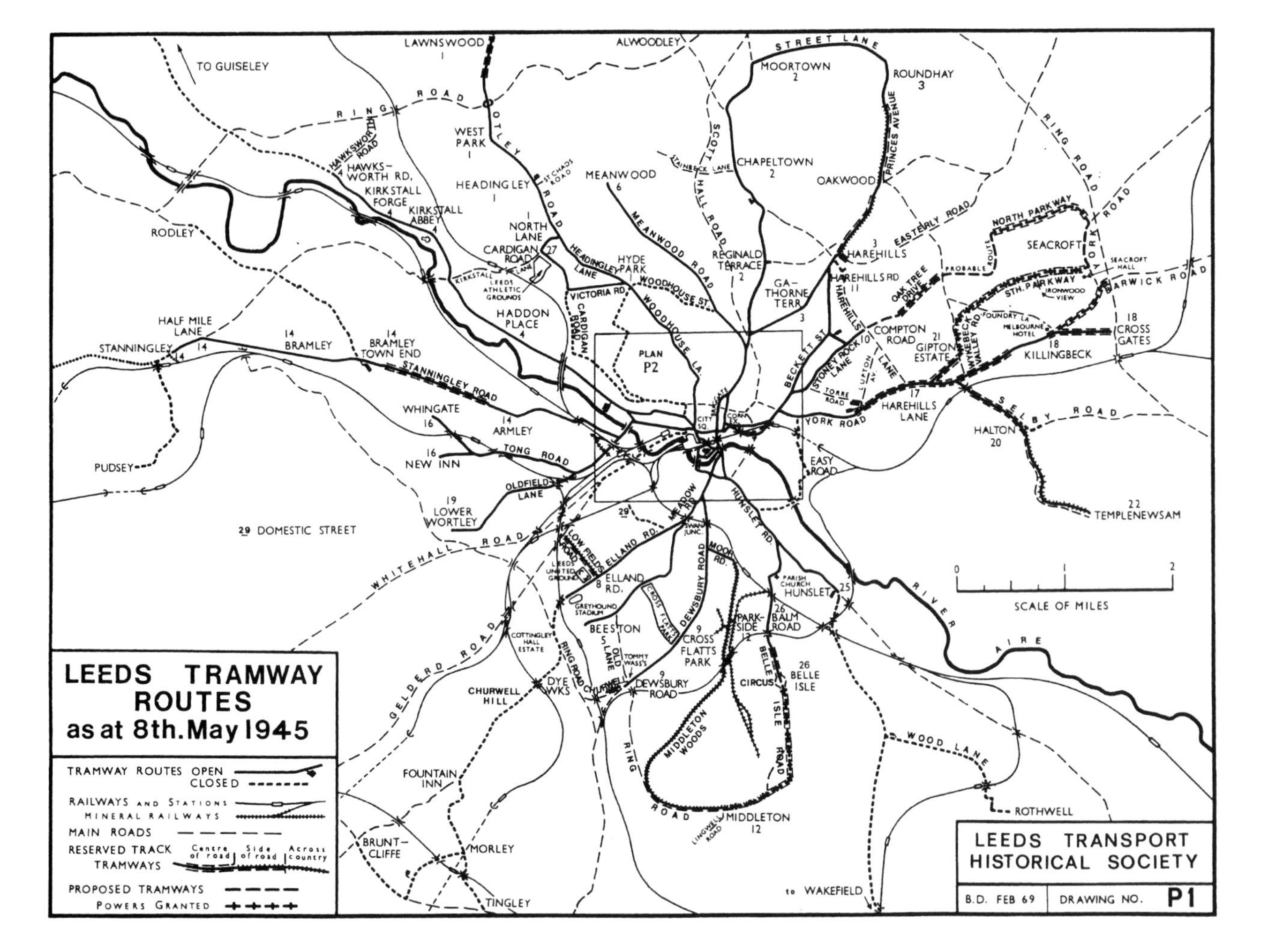

This splendid map, drawn by Bernard Donald, illustrates the general layout of the Leeds tramway system as it ran in the city in 1945. The only changes to the general area map between then and 1950 were: Beckett St-Harehills (11) and Stanley Road link to Stoney Rock Lane were abandoned, and the Tong Road-Lower Wortley route closed, on 24 August 1946; Kirkstall Abbey to Hawksworth Road closed on 3 December 1949; and Victoria Road to Cardigan Road closed on 7 December 1947. Lines that opened were St Chads Road spur (Headingley) in 1949; Stainbeck Lane spur (Chapeltown) on 7 July 1948; and Belle Isle to Middleton, on 24 August 1949.

LEEDS
in the age of the tram
1950-59

Graham H. E. Twidale

with photographs by Keith Terry MBE

Foreword by Alan Bennett

• THE NOSTALGIA OF BRITAIN •

from

The NOSTALGIA *Collection*

First published in 1991 as *A Nostalgic Look at Leeds Trams since 1950*
New edition in this format first published 2003

British Library Cataloguing in Publication Data

A catalogue record for this book is available from the British Library.

ISBN 1 85794 187 X

Silver Link Publishing Ltd
The Trundle
Ringstead Road
Great Addington
Kettering
Northants NN14 4BW

Tel/Fax: 01536 330588
email: sales@nostalgiacollection.com
Website: www.nostalgiacollection.com

Printed and bound in Great Britain

A Silver Link book
from
The NOSTALGIA *Collection*

ACKNOWLEDGEMENTS

To produce a photographic book with an historical theme requires a fair amount of research and delving into records and archives. This always needs the help and advice of others, and this book has proved to be no exception.

Two people, however, deserve a special mention. Keith Terry, many of whose collection of black and white negatives appear in the book, has been a veritable tower of strength. His knowledge of Leeds Tramways is quite phenomenal and his recollections have been both vivid and fascinating. I am grateful to him also for his valuable contribution to the captions and guidance on the 'Brief History' section. In the 2003 Queen's Birthday Honours List he was awarded the MBE for his work on tramways, etc.

My great friend Nigel Harris, whose original drive and impetus was inspirational in getting the original 'A Nostalgic Look at...' series of books under way, was invaluable, using his expertise in reading my text and 'fine tuning' it where necessary.

My thanks also go to the local history section of Leeds City Library, together with Messrs Joshua Tetley & Son Ltd, Yorkshire Bank plc, Burton Retail Group, John Crockatt Ltd, W. Brayshay & Sons Ltd, Samuel Smith (Tadcaster) Ltd, and Leeds United Football Club, all of whom provided useful information for which I am grateful.

For reproducing absolutely first-class prints from historical negatives, much credit is due to Peter Skelton of Gloucester.

The Leeds Transport Historical Society, and particularly Jim Soper and Bernard Donald, deserve a special mention for the historical maps.

For additional information I am deeply indebted to Eric T. Smith.

Finally, yet again – it seems to be becoming a habit – thanks to my wife Kendal and my two boys Matthew and Alastair (who seem to have grown up on a diet of tram nostalgia!) for their fortitude and patience while I buried myself away, fully occupied with the writing of the book.

Contents

Bibliography

Carter, Oliver *An Illustrated History of British Railway Hotels 1838-1983*
Linstrum, Derek West *Yorkshire Architects and Architecture*
Soper, J. *Leeds Transport*, Volumes 1-3
Preedy, Robert E. *Leeds Cinemas Remembered*
Leeds Theatres Remembered
Young, Andrew D. *Leeds Trams 1932-1959*
One Hundred Years of Leeds Tramways

A Guide to the City of Leeds, Handbook, 1960
City of Leeds Handbook, 1947/48
Halliwell's Film Guide
Leeds Yearbook, 1938
Yorkshire Evening Post, various issues

The splendid lines of the background buildings form a perfect background as 'Horsfield' car No 190 negotiates the junction of Briggate and Duncan Street on 24 June 1956. Former London 'Feltham' car No 513 is about to swing sharp left en route to Elland Road; this often proved to be a tricky manoeuvre, as any unsuspecting traffic pausing at the lights and intending to go straight over the junction could suddenly find the vast bulk of a tram lurching to the left in front of it. *A. K. Terry*

Above A well-known 'picture postcard' scene: this is the top of 'Lower' Briggate on Midsummer Day 1955 with 'Horsfield' car No 235 about to turn into Duncan Street on its way to Meanwood. *A. K. Terry*

Right Briggate again, the nearest Leeds ever got to a major tramway junction, between Briggate, Boar Lane and Duncan Street. However, by the time this shot was taken, on 28 September 1957, the lines to the left and those cutting straight across 154's path were no longer in use.

'Horsfield' car No 154 (one of four built by Leeds City Tramways at Kirkstall Road Works in 1930) clatters its way over the crossing on the last day of service 9 to Dewsbury Road ('Crescent' was a short-working of this route, and referred to the cinema of that name on Dewsbury Road, which had opened on 1 August 1921 and was closed as a cinema on 13 July 1968 to become a bingo hall). Note the Leeds City Police box on the island and the clock on the wire support pole – this was primarily there for the benefit of tram crews. Hepworth's is in the process of opening new premises on the right, while John Collier is on the left – they had taken over 'The Fifty Shilling Tailors' name in 1954, and were themselves subsequently taken over by Burton's in 1985. The Ford van on the right belongs to Andrew Fraser & Co, who were manufacturers/suppliers of 'Mono radial and Deri-sine (!) hydraulic pumps and valves'. *A. K. Terry*

Foreword by Alan Bennett

There was a point during the Second World War when my father took up the double bass. To recall the trams of my boyhood is to be reminded particularly of that time.

It is around 1942 and we are living in the house my parents bought when they got married, 12 Halliday Place in Upper Armley. The Hallidays are handily situated for two tram routes, and if we are going into town, rather than to Grandma's in Wortley, the quickest way is to take a number 14. This means a walk across Ridge Road, down past the back of Christ Church (and Miss Marsden's the confectioner's) to Stanningley Road. Stanningley Road is already a dual carriageway because the tram tracks, running down the middle of the road, are pebbled and enclosed by railings, so splitting what little

traffic there is into lanes. The Stanningley trams are generally somewhat superior to those on other routes, more upholstered, and when the more modern streamlined variety comes in after the war, you are more likely to see them on this route than elsewhere. But the drawback with the Stanningley Road trams is that they are coming down from Bramley or even Rodley, and are always pretty crowded, so more often than not we go for the other route, the number 16, which means walking up Moorfield Road to Charleycake Park and Whingate Junction.

This being the terminus, the tram is empty and as likely as not waiting, or, if we've just missed one, the next one will be already in sight, swaying up Whingate. We wait as the driver swings outside and with a great twang hauls the bogey over ready for the journey back, while upstairs the conductor strolls down the aisle, reversing the seats before winding back the indicator on the front. The driver and conductor then get off and have their break sat on the form by the tramstop, the driver generally older and more solid than the conductor, or, I suppose, the conductress, though I don't recall conductresses coming in until after the war.

Dad is a smoker so we troop upstairs rather than going 'inside', the word a reminder of the time when upstairs was also outside. On some trams in 1942 it still is, because in these early years of the war you can still find the odd open-ended tram. We wedge ourselves in the front corner, an unexpected treat to be exposed to the wind and weather, and also an antidote to the travel sickness from which both my brother and I suffer, though I realise now that this must have been as much due to all the smoking that went on as the motion of the tram itself. Neither of us actually is sick, but it's not uncommon and somewhere on the tram is a bin of sand just in case.

So the four of us, Mam, Dad, my brother and me, are ensconced on the tram sailing down Tong Road into town or, if we are going to see Grandma, who lives in the Gilpins, we get off half way at Fourteenth Avenue, the tramstop pictured on page 38.

Around 1942, though, we come into the double bass period when some of our tram journeys become fraught with embarrassment. Dad is a good amateur violinist, largely self-taught, so taking up the double bass isn't such a big step. He practices in the front room, which is never used for anything else, and I suppose because the bass never has the tune, it sounds terrible; he sounds as if he's sawing, which he also does, actually, as one of his other hobbies is fretwork. Though the instrument is large, the repertoire is small except in one area: swing. Until now Dad has never had much time for swing or popular music generally. His idea of a good time is to turn on the Home Service and play along with the hymns on Sunday Half Hour, or (more tentatively) with the light classics that are the staple of Albert Sandler and his Palm Court Orchestra. But now with Dad in the grip of this new craze, Mam, my brother and I are made to gather round the wireless, tuned these days to the Light Programme, so that we can listen to dance band music.

'Listen, Mam. Do you hear the beat? That's the bass. That'll be me.'

Dad has joined a part-time dance band. Even at eight years old I know that this is not a very good idea and just another of his crazes (the fretwork, the home-made beer), schemes Dad has thought up to make a bit of money. So now we are walking up Moorfield Road to get the tram again, only this time to go and watch Dad play in his band somewhere in Wortley, and our carefree family of four has been joined by a fifth, a huge and threatening cuckoo, the double bass.

Knowing what is to happen, the family make no attempt to go upstairs, but scuttle inside while Dad begins to negotiate with the conductor. The conductor spends a lot of his time in the little cubby hole under the winding metal stairs. There's often a radiator here that he perches on, and it's also where hangs the bell pull, in those days untouchable by passengers, though it's often no fancier than a knotted leather thong. In his cubby hole the conductor keeps his tin box with his spare tickets and other impedimenta which at the end of the journey he will carry down to the other end of the tram. The niche that protects the conductor from the passengers is also just about big enough to protect the double bass, but when Dad suggests this there is invariably an argument, which he never wins, the clincher generally coming when the conductor points out that strictly speaking 'that thing' isn't allowed on the tram at all.

So while we sit inside and pretend he isn't with us, Dad stands on the platform grasping the bass by the neck as if he's about to give a solo. He gets in the way of the conductor, he gets in the way of the people getting on and getting off; always a mild man, it must have been more embarrassing for him than it ever was for us. Happily this dance band phase, like the fretwork and the herb beer, doesn't last long. He gets bored with the fretwork, the herb beer regularly explodes in the larder, and the double bass is eventually advertised in the Miscellaneous column of the Evening Post and we go back to sitting on the top deck again.

After the war we move to Far Headingley where Dad, having worked all his life for the Co-op, now has a shop of his own just below the tram sheds opposite St Chad's. We live over the shop so I sleep and wake to the sound of trams; trams getting up speed for the hill before Weetwood Lane, trams spinning down from West Park, trams shunted around in the sheds in the middle of the night, the scraping of wheels, the clanging of the bell.

It is not just the passage of time that makes me invest the trams of those days with such pleasure. To be on a tram sailing down Headingley Lane on a fine evening lifts the heart at the time just as it does in memory. I go to school by tram, the fare a halfpenny from St Chad's to the Ring Road. A group of us at the Modern School scorn school dinners and come home for lunch, catching the tram from another terminus at West Park. We are all keen on music and go every Saturday to hear the Yorkshire Symphony Orchestra in the Town Hall, and it is on a tram at West Park that another sixth-former, 'Fanny' Fielder, sings to me the opening bars of Brahms's Second Piano Concerto, which I've never heard and which the YSO is playing the coming Saturday. Trams come into that too, because after the concert many of the musicians go home by tram (though none with a double bass), sitting there, rather shabby and ordinary and often with tab ends in their mouths, worlds away from the Delius, Walton and Vaughan Williams which they have been playing. It's a first lesson to me that art doesn't have much to do with appearances, and that ordinary middle-aged men in raincoats can be instruments of the sublime.

Odd details about trams come back to me now, like the slatted platforms, brown with dust, that are slung underneath either end, like some urban cowcatcher; or the little niche in the glass of the window on the seat facing the top of the stairs so that you could slide it open and hang out; and how convivial trams were, the seats reversible so that if you chose you could make up a four whenever you wanted.

How they work is always a mystery. As a child I have difficulty in understanding that the turning motion the driver makes with the handle is what drives the tram, seeming more like mixing than driving. And then there is the imposing demeanour of the ticket inspectors, invested with a spurious grandeur on a par with the one-armed man who shows you to your seat in Schofield's Cafe, or the manager of the Cottage Road cinema in his dinner jacket, or gents' outfitters in general.

I don't recall anyone ever collecting tram numbers, but the route numbers had a certain mystique, the even numbers slightly superior to the odd, which tended to belong to trams going to Gipton, Harehills, or Belle Isle, parts of Leeds where I'd never ventured. And Kirkstall will always be 4, just as Lawnswood is 1.

Buses have never inspired the same affection, too comfortable and cushioned to have a moral dimension. Trams were bare and bony, transport reduced to its basic elements, and they had a song to sing, which buses never did. I was away at university when they started to phase them out, Leeds as always in too much of a hurry to get to the future, and so doing the wrong thing. I knew at the time that it was a mistake, just as Beeching was a mistake, and that life was starting to get nastier. If trams ever come back, though, they should come back not as curiosities nor, God help us, as part of the heritage, but as a cheap and sensible way of getting from point A to point B, and with a bit of poetry thrown in.

INTRODUCTION

The subject of this book is the trams that ran in Leeds during their final nine years until their demise one cold, foggy night in November 1959. The main period of coverage is since 1950, although there are one or two references to earlier times to provide a general background. It must be stressed that this publication is in no way intended to be a definitive history of the Leeds tramway system, nor is it designed purely for the enthusiast. Those wishing to delve deeper into these aspects should avail themselves of copies of *One Hundred Years of Leeds Tramways* and *Leeds Trams 1932-1959*, both by Andrew D. Young, and *Leeds Transport*, Volumes 1-3, by Jim Soper, all of which are phenomenally detailed publications and well worth more than a glance.

It is hoped that this book will give great pleasure to those not only interested in trams, but also the folk who knew the Leeds of the recent past and who, perhaps at the time, took the trams for granted. They will, hopefully, now look back with affection to scenes and times gone for ever.

Leeds and Sheffield were the two major operators of tramway systems in Yorkshire, the latter city soldiering on for almost a further year after Leeds to become the last 'real' city street tramway in England. This distinction is important for, in Scotland, Glasgow still had many routes operating in 1959 and would continue to have an albeit steadily declining tram service until 4 September 1962.

It began in Leeds in 1871 when horse-drawn trams took to the streets, the first route being from Boar Lane to Headingley 'Oak'. A venture with steam trams lasted a few years, but the most notable event to occur was on 29 October 1891 when Leeds became the first city in the United Kingdom to operate on the streets an electrical overhead wire system. This ran from Sheepscar to Roundhay, and more details can be found in the 'Brief History' section of the book.

In the years following 1959, when the trams passed into history, Leeds has changed tremendously in many ways. Many scenes and buildings depicted in the photographs exist now in memory only, having been razed to the ground and replaced by modern equivalents or, in other cases, motorway links and inter-urban highways. Indeed, Leeds prided itself on being 'Motorway City of the Seventies', even including this boast on franked mail. I have therefore included one or two 'then and now' shots to give a comparison of just how much things have changed.

Like other cities, Leeds had perhaps more than its fair share of soot-blackened buildings, only to be expected in a great industrial and commercial centre. Many factory chimneys dominated the skyline and, together with the myriad of household fires burning in countless grates, they contributed a great deal to the Lowryesque landscape that has all but gone today. It is strange to reflect that, at a time when factory and household chimneys were pumping thousands more tons of sulphur dioxide and fumes into the atmosphere than today, the Scandinavian pine forests seemed to thrive and we didn't seem to hear of acid rain. I wonder why?

Many city centre buildings have now been cleaned, taking on a new lease of life, but sadly, in some cases, other fine ones were demolished. Anyone returning to the city today who had been away for the last 40 years would hardly recognise some parts. Shopping malls and precincts were still far-off dreams – in the 1950s, corner shops abounded and the ubiquitous Co-op could be seen in all parts of the city.

I am sure many readers will recall visiting the Co-op and other shops like it, and enjoying the aroma of freshly ground coffee, seeing the slabs of butter waiting to be cut into half-pound 'pats', buying sugar in 2lb blue bags (remember Mr Cube?) and, when you asked for a 'packet of Kelloggs', the assistant (remember them?) knew instantly that you meant cornflakes! This was also the time when small boys delivered groceries to your home on big shop bikes complete with large basket – truly a thing of the past.

Other famous shop names to be seen in the photographs that have now gone the way of all flesh include the Home & Colonial Stores, the

Maypole, Thrift Stores and The Fifty Shilling Tailors – later to become John Collier, 'The window to watch'.

The far more hurried and increasingly stressful times of the next 40 years were still to come. Change had taken place slowly since the war and people were adjusting at a steady pace; Prime Minister Harold Macmillan's 'wind of change', which at that time referred to the changing British Empire, particularly in Africa, had still to start in earnest.

Cinemas were still found in abundance, with many choices of film on offer. In 1938 there were no fewer than 71 cinemas in Leeds, including premises licensed for cinematograph entertainment. Their wonderful names included the Coliseum in Cookridge Street (which was the largest, seating 2,731 persons), the Cosy, Electra, Haddon Hall, Philosophical (!) Hall, Picturedrome, and the Tatler in Boar Lane – this was the smallest and seated just 300 customers. Many of these cinemas had, of course, gone by the end of the 1950s, but before television (not to mention bingo) tightened its stranglehold, one could visit them to see an enormous variety of offerings ranging from 'A stupendous, colossal Biblical epic' down to some 'Creature from the Black Lagoon'. Happy days!

Housing was then, as now, a major item on any Council's agenda, Leeds being no exception. New estates were springing up across a wide area, or existing developments were being enlarged, in a post-war boom the like of which has not been seen since. If someone at the time had suggested to the City Fathers that they would one day be selling council houses to their tenants, they would have treated the idea with incredulity.

In the course of compiling this book, I have read some wonderful publications, particularly official handbooks, which give a fascinating insight into how Leeds thrived throughout the 1950s. I suppose the city's foremost claim to fame rests with the wool, textile and clothing industries. Well-known and famous names around at that time included W. E. Yates Ltd, Fred Lodge & Sons, Henry Lister & Sons, James Mather & Sons and, of course, Montague Burton, a list that merely scratches the surface of a tremendous clothing manufacturing empire whose fame was known throughout the world.

A close second to the clothing trade was, and still is, engineering – especially locomotive-building – with names like Kirkstall Forge, Catton & Co, Thomas Smith (Rodley) Ltd, Fairbairn Lawson and Thomas Green & Son, who became part of the Blackburn & General Aircraft Group in 1951 – many readers will recall their lawnmowers. Locomotive-builders included Hudswell Clarke, Fowler, and Hunslet Engine Co, with general engineers C. R. Tipping & Co, Charles H. Roe (with both aircraft and bus associations), Blakeys Boot Protectors, and George Depledge being just a few from what was a lengthy list.

The volume of traffic using the city streets was considerably less than today, particularly in outlying districts. The private car was still out of many people's reach and it would be some years before suburban streets (which were never intended to carry present-day traffic) would become choked with parked vehicles despite striped single, broken or double yellow lines! The photographs in this book vividly evoke the mood and feelings of those times, with many favourite old models of car, van (remember the Jowett/Bradford?) and lorry gracing the scene. It is also interesting to note that many views show an almost complete absence of vehicular traffic – not to mention litter!

Public transport in Leeds, as everywhere else, was then still heavily used by the community. In 1950 the tramway system was, by and large, still intact and ran to many districts of the city. Some routes had been closed before the war, principally those outside the city boundary or with extensive single-line operation. In addition, soon after hostilities ceased and more buses became available, the single-line and passing-loop routes along Victoria Road and Cardigan Road (27), to Harehills Road via Beckett Street (11), and Lower Wortley via Oldfield Lane (19) were closed.

That apart, things seemed as if they were likely to go on at a comparatively leisurely pace for many years to come. Recovery after the war was slow, and while modernisation was taking place, it was at nothing like the breakneck speed to which we are accustomed today. For example, the city streets were, apart from the centre and most main roads, still lit by almost 20,000 gas lamps in 1950. Many readers will, I know, have fond childhood memories of these lamps; one could have great fun swinging from a rope attached to the bracket or banging the posts at dusk to make them come on earlier! Their warm, spluttering, yellow glow after dark is now so very reminiscent of a bygone era. Goodness knows how many men were employed to travel the streets weekly to wind up the clocks, clean the glass and replace mantles where necessary.

Fashions, of course, immediately date any photograph, and those shown here are no exception. Generally speaking a crowd of people looked fairly drab, particularly during inclement weather, when the ubiquitous gabardine mackintosh, much in evidence within these pages, came into its own. Indeed, one tends to think that everyone then wore

An evocative scene in Briggate on a busy Saturday afternoon, 28 September 1957. Briggate is Leeds's main shopping street even today, but no traffic at all is permitted. Until the late-1950s there were no regular bus services along this street (just as there were no trams along The Headrow), although occasional buses were used to supplement trams to Roundhay Park on a busy day. Even so, most buses to and from the Park were operated from City Square or Vicar Lane.

'Feltham' No 529 is on its way to Dewsbury Road; this was to be the last day that the No 9 trams would operate. No 529 was one of the four cars of this class to be selected to trial a diamond pantograph current collector in March 1951. However, the experiment was not considered a success and the cars quickly reverted to bow collectors, as shown here. A Ford V8 Pilot, Morris Minor, Hillman, Austin A30 and A35 van complete the scene, together with either a Lambretta or Vespa scooter. *A. K. Terry*

Above It is 9.40am on a quiet Sunday morning, 4 April 1954, at the familiar location of Briggate, Boar Lane and Duncan Street. All the shops are closed, this being many, many years before Sunday opening became common. Indeed, it would have been considered unthinkable in 1954.

The newspaper seller is taking advantage of the vacant entrance to Saxone Shoes and seems to be doing a brisk trade. On display is a board advertising the *Sunday Dispatch*, now but a memory together with its sister paper the *Daily Dispatch*. Other newspapers that have disappeared since this time include the *Daily Graphic*, *News Chronicle* and *Sunday Pictorial*. The Briggate tramcar loading barriers are shown here to good effect as 'Showboat' No 161 makes her way to Harehills. To board a tram at the barriers at the driving end of the tram was, to the unfamiliar traveller, something of a novelty. *R. Wiseman*

Right A sombre young Leeds City policeman casts a wary eye over the scene at Briggate junction on 3 March 1956. This would be the last day that trams would run to Lawnswood, where 'Horsfield' car No 197, swinging into Boar Lane, is heading, although the rear destination screen clearly shows 'Crossgates'. The handles for the upper deck destination screens were very tempting for the hands of inquisitive children, although it would have taken some effort to wind it from 'Lawnswood' to 'Crossgates'. At this time both City and Central stations flourished, as did Alexandre the Tailors. Central Station is gone but the Alexandre building survives in commercial use.

The young boy crossing Briggate is so very typical of the time with his cap, blue gabardine, shorts and long (if somewhat wrinkled!) socks. Pedestrians accepted the trams as a part of daily life and it is strange that there is a good deal of fuss today about putting them back on the streets. *A. K. Terry*

much the same type of garments but, on reflection, nothing has really changed – other than brighter colours. Certainly dress materials today lack the clean, fresh look of those in the 1940s and 1950s. Perhaps we have come full circle, as anoraks, 'shell suits' and expensive designer trainers have merely taken over as the modern 'dress'.

Tram crews generally wore the full uniform and looked much the better for it. How smart they looked with peaked caps, shirts and ties and polished shoes. There was certainly a considerable pride in the job then.

In 1953, the year of the Queen's Coronation, the first major route closure of the decade took place. This was No 14 from the Corn Exchange to Half Mile Lane, on which the last car ran on 3 October; the route had, until 3 December 1938, continued on into Pudsey. This represented the first of the planned closures aimed at eventually removing all trams from the city, culminating in the withdrawal of services Nos 17, 18, 20 and 22 along York Road on 7 November 1959.

On that final night an official procession of ten 'Horsfield' cars, two of them illuminated, set off from Swinegate depot at 6.15pm. The first five went to Cross Gates, the remainder to Temple Newsam, after which the convoy reassembled at Selby Road junction and returned to Swinegate at around 7.15pm. After 88 years of various forms of tramway, operations had come to an end and the system passed into the history books.

Readers may notice that many of the Leeds scenes show the tram rails laid in asphalt rather than granite setts. This was not as hard-wearing or resilient but provided a more comfortable ride for the motorist – not to mention the cyclist. In addition, although trams generally were blamed for causing unnecessary traffic congestion, particularly in city centres, the Leeds system utilised many miles of reserved track that took them completely away from other road users, thus causing no hindrance at all.

It is somewhat ironic that, after more than 40 years, trams are now to return to the city. They have been established elsewhere, notably in Croydon, Manchester, Sheffield, the West Midlands and Nottingham, and they should be back on the streets of Leeds by 2007. There are comments elsewhere to indicate that modern trams will be back on the same streets as those in individual pictures, but doubtless the backgrounds, the fashions and, of course, the corner shops will have changed.

My own memories of Leeds trams go back to school days when visiting relatives in Chapeltown after travelling by train from Blackpool or catching a No 18, 20 or 22 up to the Shaftesbury Cinema at the corner of Harehills Lane and York Road, walking down Osmondthorpe Lane and taking in the heady delights of Neville Hill motive power depot – railway engines had a similar fascination for me! Standing at Briggate barriers and boarding the tram at the driver's end always seemed a novelty and remains a vivid memory to this day. It all seems so very far away now, but looking at the photographs makes it appear as though it was just yesterday. I hope many of you agree.

The noise of squealing wheel flanges as the cars negotiated a particularly tight curve, the thrill of a fast run around the Middleton circle, a trip to Roundhay Park on a glorious summer's day, the distinctive hum and rumble of a 'Horsfield' car as it pottered along Street Lane, or the unmistakable noise from four- and eight-wheelers as they thundered over Briggate junction with the accompanying hiss of the bow collector, all evoke memories of sounds and experiences sometimes perhaps long forgotten.

Unless otherwise noted, all the photographs in the book are from Keith Terry's collection, and many had never been published before the appearance of the original, 'A Nostalgic Look at...' volume. Study each picture carefully. Look at the motor vehicles, the clothing fashions, and the familiar shops that have disappeared. Are the advertisements on the trams and hoardings familiar today? See how many different beers there were to delight the drinker! Even the people, as individuals, seem to have changed; yet you may see yourself or a relative or friend captured for all time in that split-second when the camera clicked.

If the book gives you as much pleasure to read as it gave me to prepare, it will all have been worthwhile.

A BRIEF HISTORY OF LEEDS TRAMWAYS

The word 'brief' must here be taken quite literally, for the history of any transport system is both complex and diverse. Others with far more experience and knowledge of detail than me have written comprehensive volumes (listed in the Bibliography) explaining the intricacies and complicated problems that combined to create the Leeds tramway system. I am particularly indebted to Andrew D. Young, whose publications are mentioned in the Bibliography, for granting permission to use information and quote passages from his books.

A horse bus service first took to the streets of Leeds in 1839, running to 'The Three Horse Shoes' in Headingley. Over the years several other routes opened and horse buses ran until 1911, when the service from Lower Wortley to Old Farnley ceased.

However, we are really concerned with the trams. Their story starts in 1869-70 with the passing of the Leeds Tramway Order conferred on promoters William and David Busby, permitting the construction of five horse tram routes. The very first route opened on 16 September 1871 and ran from Boar Lane to Headingley 'Oak'.

The Leeds Tramways Company took over the powers to run the tramways in 1872 and subsequently introduced several other routes, including those to Kirkstall, Hunslet, Chapeltown and Meanwood. By the end of 1879 it was possible to wait no more than 10 minutes for the next horse tram to come along. It would be good to have such a frequency today on many bus routes!

A major development occurred in 1877 when the first experimental steam trams arrived on the scene. These were built by Kitson & Co in Leeds and were considered satisfactory apart from their emission of grit and fumes, which caused some discomfort to passengers and, I suspect, to many other road users and pedestrians! They eventually became well known on the Headingley and Wortley routes and it was a common sight to see the small steam engines towing double-deck trailer cars among the multitude of horse-drawn vehicular traffic sharing the road.

However, the steam trams were heavy and tended to do much damage to the rails, which were only designed to carry the much lighter horse trams. The type of rail was subsequently changed and the problem of excessive wear was reduced, but by 1890 it was clear from experience elsewhere that electricity was going to be the power of the future for municipal tramways. Blackpool had commenced using electric trams in 1885, and still does so today.

In 1890 the Corporation was approached by an American named Graff Baker, representing the American Thomson Houston Company, who offered to rebuild the Roundhay route (Sheepscar to Roundhay) for electric traction using overhead cable. The company was given permission to carry out the proposal; the line was subsequently electrified and the company also provided six cars to work it.

On 29 October 1891 came the great day when the system, unique in the United Kingdom, began operation. It was the forerunner of what was to become a large and vigorous undertaking for the next 88 years in the city – never mind the rest of the world!

Fares in the early days were not particularly cheap (a 2d minimum being commonplace) and the companies that ran the various bus and tram routes tended to serve the more affluent areas of the city where most profit could be made. It was not until after 1894, when Leeds Corporation took over the running rights from the various companies, that things began to improve and routes were introduced to stimulate the growth of population in underdeveloped and working-class areas rather than relying solely on the existing affluently populated parts of the city.

The last horse tram on the Whitehall Road route ran in October 1901 and the last steam tram from Bramley into the city in April 1902, following which much electrification of routes took place. The Roundhay Park route was closed in 1896 and re-opened and extended through the city to Kirkstall Abbey in the following year. By 1905 electric trams were running to many parts of the city, and by 1908 the tram fleet had expanded to some 282 passenger vehicles, with various works cars adding to the system.

A modernisation programme was begun in 1910 to update vehicles by fitting vestibules and top covers. The electric cars' original livery of blue and white was replaced by primrose and chocolate, with fleet numbers so large that a particular car could be identified from far away.

Lines running outside the city boundary were constructed to places such as Morley, Pudsey, Rodley, Rothwell and Guiseley. It was also possible to travel by tram to Wakefield using cars of the West Riding Tramways Co, and to Bradford. The latter's tramway gauge was 4 feet compared with the standard gauge of 4ft 8½in used by Leeds; where the two tracks met at Stanningley Bottoms, the unique dual-gauge cars used by the two cities had either to increase or decrease their wheel gauge depending on which way the car was travelling. Specially adapted trucks were fitted to both cities' cars, enabling the gauge to be changed as required with the assistance of a travelling fitter. This incredible piece of engineering was not entirely successful, and through running ceased on 25 March 1918 after just 11 years of spasmodic, interrupted service.

Many of the trams that ran in Leeds were built at the tramways' own workshops in Kirkstall Road. These survived as the principal location for building, rebuilding and major overhauling of trams until their closure on 7 November 1957, after which time any other work necessary on the then dwindling fleet of cars was undertaken by Swinegate Depot.

Leeds, together with Bradford, also became involved with experiments with trolleybuses, sometimes referred to as 'trackless trams'. Trolleybus services ran between Guiseley, Otley and Burley in Wharfedale until 1928, and between City Square and Whitehall Road (Farnley) until 1926. Trolleybuses in Bradford survived until 26 March 1972, the last such undertaking in the United Kingdom.

But it was in the 1920s that the tramcar in Britain generally was enjoying its heyday, Leeds being no exception. The most noteworthy development of this period was the Middleton Light Railway, the main portion of which opened on 12 November 1925. This was a tremendous operation that could easily have a whole chapter to itself; space, unfortunately, only permits a shortened version. Briefly, Leeds Corporation bought a considerable portion of land from the Middleton Colliery Company, principally for council house construction, the first being ready for occupation in 1920. To quote from Andrew D. Young's book, *Leeds Trams 1932-1959*:

> 'In December 1923, Leeds ordered 16,800 sleepers, 6,000 tons of slag ballast, 56 tons of tie bars, 1,750 tons of rail and 67,000 rail chips for the new line, plus nine miles of trolley wire. Starting at Moor Road they laid 3.63 miles of double sleeper track with centre poles running alongside the colliery railway to a point near the ex-GNR Beeston goods branch and then curving away on its own rising 300 feet in 1½ scenic miles to a 473-foot summit at the Middleton water tower. Rejoining the road here, it ran on a wide grass verge next to Middleton Park Road, ending opposite the north-south axis of the estate; a further short extension was made in 1927.
>
> The main portion was brought into use on 12 November 1925 after a formal opening two days earlier, and thus did Leeds obtain one of the finest tram routes ever built in Britain. From then on, the Middleton Light Railway was a major factor in the continued development of the city's tramways.'

Other sections of reserved track included that from Harehills to Oakwood (and later on to Roundhay) out to Cross Gates, long stretches of York Road, Selby Road and Stanningley Road, and from Halton to Temple Newsam.

In 1922 it was felt by the Transport Department that some sort of upgrading of the trams was required. Open balcony cars were still a common sight, and it was time to modernise and have totally enclosed cars. A requirement for 200 modern trams was jointly

The last of the 'Convert' cars (those that had been converted from open balcony cars), No 359 was first made into the 'Festival of Britain' tram in 1951 – hence the globe (which revolved as the tram progressed along the road). It was used for various future events in all manner of disguises, the globe being retained, although probably looking a little incongruous on occasions. The car was painted in many guises, sometimes with the aid of the local College of Art. No 359 is seen here on 24 April 1955 in Chapeltown Depot encouraging people to invest in National Savings, which at that time was still very much part of the Post Office. *A. K. Terry*

placed with Brush Electrical Engineering, English Electric and the Department's own workshops.

The new cars were subsequently known as 'Pivotal' or 'Chamberlain' cars (named after the General Manager from 1925-28, William C. Chamberlain). The idea behind the pivotal truck was to make a four-wheel car run like an eight-wheel bogie car – that is, by allowing the four wheels to turn when the car traversed a curve.

Much could be written about the pivotal cars but space does not permit. There are various schools of thought as to how these cars really performed. To some they were fine, particular when new and in first-class condition. To others they were poor and rode very roughly. It is probably fair to say that when in need of truck maintenance they could play havoc with trackwork. Nevertheless, they were indeed good servants to the system, were sturdy workhorses and gave many years of service. Many cars, however, received a 'rigid' truck in later years, improving their riding qualities.

In 1930 there was developed and introduced what was to become one of the mainstays of the Leeds tramway fleet until its last day. This was the highly successful 'Horsfield' car – again named after the Manager of the day, Mr R. L. Horsfield. Four were constructed at Kirkstall Road Works and a further 100 were built by Brush for delivery in 1931. They were truly excellent vehicles and, though fairly basic in design and appearance, had a modern truck, air brakes, two 50hp motors, and roller-bearing axleboxes.

Thus in 1931 Leeds had over 350 cars built since 1920, making it one of the youngest fleets of trams in the country. Sadly, Mr Horsfield died suddenly in that year after only three years as Manager. He did much for the tramway undertaking for, as well as introducing the class of cars mentioned, he instigated the enlarging of Kirkstall Road Works and Swinegate Depot and the modernising of the power supply.

His successor was Mr W. Vane Morland, during whose period of office the tramways changed little. The first diesel buses arrived in 1934 and some old single-line tram routes were closed. There was also a change in the overhead system in the mid-1930s. This involved re-alignment of wires from side to centre running, and Fischer bow collector operation was then steadily introduced in place of trolley poles between 1936 and 1938.

Despite the fact that Leeds had a relatively modern fleet of trams during this period, a further new class was introduced. They were superb vehicles and subsequently became famous, known to enthusiasts as the

Above The 'Chamberlain' or 'Pivotal' car, as seen here, was the largest single type of tram in Leeds, numbering 200 in total. All were built between 1925 and 1928, and the last of the type ran in 1957. No 17 is seen here in its earlier blue and cream livery making slow progress down Wellington Street on a bright morning in May 1949, following a horse-drawn LMS railway wagon, which appears to be carrying flour.

The tram is passing the entrance to Central Station, which at that time was still a busy terminus, although the name 'Central' was something of a misnomer, and the buildings themselves did nothing to enhance its reputation. Not many mourned its passing and final closure on 29 April 1967. The gentleman on the extreme right appears to be a railway guard about to go on duty.

W. Brayshay & Sons were founded in the early 1890s and moved to premises on Wellington Street in 1930. They were, and still are, a well-known name in the wholesale carpet trade. The premises shown in the picture were badly damaged by fire in 1963 and Brayshay's moved to another part of Leeds. *A. K. Terry*

Left 'Horsfield' car No 151 was the precursor of the class that eventually numbered 104. It was built experimentally by Leeds City Tramways in 1930 and is seen here in May 1956 at the spur in Stainbeck Lane, Chapeltown. The 'Horsfield' cars were affectionately nicknamed 'Showboats' during their long service.

The Church and property in the background have since given way to a modern shopping development. Thrift Stores were very common in the 1950s and 1960s with branches all over the city – I am sure they are much missed today. *A. K. Terry*

'Middleton Bogies', but in their early life to crews and the general public as 'Bluebirds'. The prototype, No 255, emerged from the Brush Electrical Engineering Co of Loughborough in 1933. This and the 16 other examples (eight of them built by English Electric) were extremely modern and designed to the highest standards with upholstered seating (including one for the driver!), all-round upper-deck vision, twin headlamps, four 45hp motors, platform doors, and seating for 70 passengers. No 255's livery was 'electric' blue and cream, and this car was, initially, fitted with twin trolleys. The cost of building was £3,000. The cars spent most of their working lives (though not exclusively) on the Middleton route, and it is a tragedy that none survived the cutter's torch.

In 1934-35 three other similar cars with only four wheels each were built at Kirkstall Road Works. Because of their striking livery design, 'electric' blue and cream with a chevron cream band at each end, they soon became known as 'Lance Corporals'.

Tram fares in Leeds during the 1930s were extremely low. Between 1928 and 1944 there was a 2d maximum fare, which could take you anywhere from the City Centre to any point inside the city boundary. A higher fare was charged for cross-city journeys and also to points beyond the city boundary on the Guiseley, Morley and Pudsey routes. As a result the number of tram passengers soared from 160 million in 1929 to 170 million by 1939, a remarkable testament to cheap fares and a modern and reliable fleet of cars.

Plans were discussed to extend the system further to new housing estates, the prime destinations being Belle Isle and Seacroft. An extension from Balm Road to 82 Belle Isle Road did not, however, open until 22 July 1940, while the final connection with Middleton was, through various circumstances, delayed until 28 August 1949. The Seacroft extension never happened. A small branch from York Road down to Gipton was opened on 11 September 1936, the intention being to extend this up to Seacroft, but constant deferral and ultimate

One of the last 'Bluebird' cars to carry the original pale blue and cream livery was No 260, seen here about to cross 'Christ Church' junction in Meadow Lane on its way to Swinegate from Middleton. The tram still retains its triple screen indicator and protruding headlights. Note the small boy upstairs poking his head out of the window on this fine day in June 1948. What looks to be an ex-Army vehicle follows behind bearing the initials WRCAEC; despite intensive research, the explanation of these letters remains a mystery. *A. K. Terry*

withdrawal of the scheme left an interesting prospective development as just something that might have been.

A rise in the number of passengers carried in 1939 resulted in the city buying the first of an ultimately large fleet of second-hand trams from other cities. The first three to arrive were from London. They were HR/2 cars (HR standing for 'hilly route') and were renumbered in the Leeds fleet as 277, 278 and 279. They arrived without air-brakes and only the first two were subsequently fitted with them.

On the outbreak of war old balcony cars due for withdrawal had to take to the streets again. The Ministry of Transport ordered that no serviceable cars should be withdrawn anywhere in the United Kingdom in case bomb damage might affect the availability of others. Also as a result of the war, the distance between tram stops was increased from 210 to 290 yards to alleviate the wearing out of rails; it is doubtful whether all were returned to their former length after hostilities ceased.

As in other cities, wartime modifications to trams were undertaken including the fitting of headlamp masks, window netting and white paint applied to fenders, handrails and steps, which during the blackout gave some small benefit to passengers when boarding or alighting from cars. Some Leeds trams were also painted a ghastly (in my view!) all-over khaki livery. One other interesting Government directive was that trams (and buses) should not be stored in great numbers in depots overnight but should be kept at various points throughout the city to avoid possible mass destruction by bombing. Thus, many cars were stored in the open at Temple Newsam, Torre Road Depot yard, Middleton sidings at Lingwell Road, Easterly Road, and additional space in Low Fields Road. A bomb did indeed hit Swinegate Depot on 9 March 1941, causing slight damage to five trams, whereas if the depot had been full it could have been much worse.

It became obvious that more second-hand trams would be needed during the war and several were bought from Hull in 1942 and 1945. These cars were to run in their new home until 1950-51, and replaced a similar number of life-expired open balcony cars, which had to remain in store.

For the first time since 1928, and after much wrangling, the first major alteration to tram fares took place in February 1944. Things did not improve, however, either in terms of economics, labour relations or the general state of the trams and track. All this culminated in a transport strike in September/October 1945, during which members of the public were invited to keep the city's trams and buses running. This met with partial success and would be the last time in British history that members of the public would be asked to drive trams in a city. It is interesting to note that from this point onwards, virtually until the end of the system, politics seems to have played a major role in the fortunes of Leeds tramways, characterised by acrimonious antagonism and bitter debate between the two main parties as each held office.

It perhaps should be mentioned at this juncture that various new schemes, ranging from a monorail to a subway system, had been mooted by several bodies, and in 1944 a Reconstruction Committee on the Council was set up to consider post-war development. The proposed subway was to take the trams off the city centre streets. As Leeds centre was considered small for a city of its overall size and was gradually choking itself to death, the ideal way of removing public transport, in the shape of trams, was to put them underground. Again, much could be written about this idea, which was highly detailed and innovative. Suffice to say that when a new Labour Council took office in October 1945, the scheme was shelved in favour of spending money on rehousing. In many ways this was unfortunate, for it could have become a most interesting and far-reaching idea.

Leeds came through the war more or less unscathed (compared with other cities), but was in a shabby, run-down and somewhat depressing condition. The large tram fleet was serviceable but in need of much attention, as were the track and overhead equipment. However, costs were ever-increasing and any thought of modernisation had to take a back seat, although various track repairs and junction replacements did take place during this time.

More second-hand purchases of trams were made, this time from Manchester and

Above Car 275 was a 'one-off' rather boxy tram built from spare parts in 1943. Called an austerity tram, it was originally numbered 104 after the 'Chamberlain' car it replaced, which had been burned out in 1942. No 275 ran exclusively on the Bramley route when new, and is seen here in Duncan Street in August 1950 painted in a later livery of dark blue and cream. *A. K. Terry*

Below This late 1940s scene at the junction of Hunslet Lane and Meadow Lane shows two well-filled cars, Beeston 'air-brake' No 402 and an unidentified 'Convert' car, coming from either Hunslet or Belle Isle and both in blue livery. The 'Adelphi' public house dominates the background and survives to this day.

The advert on the 'Convert' proclaims 'At any time of strain or pain Genasprin gets you through'. This remedy seems to have disappeared into the mists of time, although I suspect we could all do with a dose of it today from time to time! Car 402 survived until 1951 and was by then in an all-blue livery with smaller fleet numbers. Before withdrawal it developed a 'bouncing' motion and was known to some tram crews as 'Josephine' – whether this referred to the supposed sexual proclivities of Napoleon's Josephine we shall never know! *R. Wiseman*

Southampton, when seven Manchester 'Pilcher' cars arrived in 1946 and 1948, and 30 Southampton 'Balloon' cars were ordered in 1949. It transpired that only 11 of the latter actually ran in service, the rest being in a very poor condition. They were, by and large, unsuccessful and had a very short life in Leeds, all being withdrawn by 1953.

The most important and far-reaching purchase of second-hand trams was from London. Mr V. J. Matterface, previously Senior Technical Assistant (Trams and Trolleybuses) with London Transport, came to Leeds in March 1948 as Tramways Rolling Stock Engineer, and it was at his suggestion that the purchase of ex-London 'Feltham' cars was pursued. Subsequently London Transport agreed to lend Leeds one of these trams in exchange for 17 pre-war AEC Regent buses.

Car No 2099, fresh from overhaul in Charlton Works, arrived in Leeds in October 1949. After various trials it was put on display for a week in City Square, still in its London livery. It certainly made an impression with the public and Transport Committee alike, so much so that agreement was reached to purchase all 92 of the class at a total cost of £735 per car, including delivery by Pickfords.

The main batch of 'Felthams' began to arrive in August 1950. No 2099 was renumbered 501 and the remainder numbered in sequence as they arrived. They were certainly a bargain for Leeds, being standardised, relatively speedy, with plenty of spares available and likely to give several more years' service in their new home. Two cars that were due to be transferred were burned out while in London, but their trucks and equipment were released, together with ex-LCCT car No 1, a truly superb vehicle that entered service as Leeds No 301 in December 1951. The arrival of the 'Felthams' enabled the last of the Hull cars to be withdrawn, together with other elderly Leeds cars; 68 of the 'new' trams were in service by May 1952, the other 22 being put into store while normal overhauls were undertaken.

In May 1950 it was decided to change the colours of Corporation Transport vehicles. Hitherto the buses and trams generally had been in varying shades of blue and cream, but henceforth the buses would be in, at first, three shades of green – later two – and the trams in red and cream. Various trials of livery variation took place, but at the end of 1950 a standard had been adopted that can be seen in

In 1949 Leeds Corporation agreed to purchase several former Southampton trams. It transpired that only 11 ever ran in service, while a further eight intended for service were never used, and several more, having been delivered to Leeds, were despatched immediately for use by a pig farmer at Farsley. They were basically poor cars, were never very popular with crews or public, and had a very short life in the city, the last being withdrawn in 1953. Here in May of that year, No 300 passes the University in Woodhouse Lane on its way to Lawnswood on service No 1. *A. K. Terry*

most of this book's photographs. Many regretted the passing of the blue livery, as it was fairly uncommon throughout the country, but it was felt that red would weather far better in the Leeds industrial atmosphere. This, as it turned out, was not strictly true. Between cars freshly leaving the paint shop in bright red and the time for their next repaint, the shade had changed considerably. The remaining fleet had received the new livery by April 1954.

In 1953, with the transport undertaking making another big deficit – around £230,000 – the anti-tram lobby gained ground. The *Yorkshire Evening News* (which was last printed on 3 December 1963) published a series of articles on transport that revolved around the tramway being a millstone round the Department's neck (the paper was a vociferous opponent of the trams until they were finally withdrawn).

After much political infighting during the early part of 1953, the Labour Party regained power on the Council and immediately set about implementing its policy of gradual abandonment of the tramway system. It was decided that the first route to go would be the No 14 to Stanningley, a high-loss service. This closed on 3 October 1953 and thus the inexorable scrapping of the whole system started to gain momentum.

One happier event in 1953 (apart from the Coronation and Blackpool FC winning the FA Cup!) was the introduction of two revolutionary single-deck trams, or railcars as they became known. These two cars were extremely modern vehicles with all the latest sophisticated technology of the day. Again, much space could be devoted to the story of these cars, but it is not possible here. They entered service in a spectacular livery of royal purple, cream and gold-leaf lining in early June 1953, and spent the rest of the year and some of the next making 'guest appearances' on various routes throughout the city before settling down to spend the rest of their short lives on the No 25 service to Hunslet.

One other single-decker joined 601 and 602

A busy scene at the junction of Briggate, Swinegate, Bridge End and Call Lane in June 1952. A Humber Hawk and lined-out 'Horsfield' car 163 pause at the traffic lights before proceeding to Beeston. Behind is the original 'Feltham' car to arrive in Leeds (No 2099), still in its London livery but by now renumbered 501. *A. K. Terry*

A classic shot of 'Feltham' car No 513 in the Easterly Road terminal spur outside the Clock Cinema, Harehills, in May 1952, about to work service No 4 back to Kirkstall Abbey. These fine cars were, however, very heavy and their high axle loading gave the trackwork and rail joints quite a pounding. This, in turn, played havoc with their bolster and axlebox springs. In 1952 it was decided to make one of the cars (No 519) a single-decker to lighten the load. It was soon found that it was so solidly built that conversion would be quite uneconomical in man-hours, and 519 returned to service unaltered. Hammonds Ales, a popular brew of the day, was subsequently taken over by Bass. *A. K. Terry*

on the 25. This was ex-Sunderland car No 85, which had been purchased in 1944 with a possible view to it being a precursor for the ill-fated subway system. It remained in store until 1949, when conversion work was started, with the intention of it being used as a prototype vehicle for twin-car operation. This interesting idea unfortunately came to nothing and the car eventually entered service as No 600 as late as August 1954, 10 years after it arrived in Leeds.

At the beginning of the decade there were four tram depots, at Chapeltown, Headingley, Torre Road and Swinegate. With the gradual closure of routes, by November 1955 only Swinegate was left, which eventually undertook repairs and paint touch-ups. Of the 22 remaining 'Felthams' that had arrived in 1951, only 15 were put into service, the last, No 582, on 31 July 1956.

There is now little left to relate. Route withdrawals went on at a relentless pace, the final abandonment date being eventually brought forward from 1962 to November 1959. During 1955, 1956 and 1957 many routes disappeared, including those to Lawnswood, Meanwood, Whingate and New Inn, Beeston and Dewsbury Road. The last car also ran through City Square on 7 November 1957, the night Kirkstall Road Works closed.

At the beginning of 1959 only services Nos 3, 12, 17, 18, 20, 22, 25, 26 and 27 survived, serving areas including Middleton, Belle Isle, Moortown, Halton, Cross Gates, Temple Newsam and Hunslet. Only when the Briggate barriers were demolished in March 1959 and the trams to Moortown were withdrawn, did it finally sink in with many people that the end was very close.

What remained of the system staggered on throughout the glorious summer of 1959. The cars themselves were looking shabby, worn-out and battle-scarred. There was an all-pervading air of finality and it seemed as though few now really cared.

An official procession took place on Saturday 7 November 1959 with cars journeying for the last time on what was left of a once superb system with its miles of reserved track. The procession was all over by 7.30pm, the last car entered Swinegate Depot and another page of history was turned.

Very little tangible evidence is left of the trams today. Several wire support poles can be seen here and there, particularly in Street Lane, Roundhay Road and Stanningley Road. Most of the tram depot buildings are still to be seen though in different guises – Swinegate Depot, which later became the Queen's Hall, has since been demolished.

However, when trams return to the city we shall have come full circle and once more the streets of Leeds will echo to the sound of the tram, albeit in a much modernised form.

Top Charles H. Roe Ltd railcar No 602 is seen here on its first day of public service, 1 June 1953. As a goodwill gesture for the Coronation, free rides were given to all passengers. With sister car 601, these two railcars were extremely modern, incorporating much 1950s 'state of the art' equipment. One item that proved unpopular in later times, however, was the fact that there was only seating for 34 with additional room for 36 standing. No 602 is seen here at the north crossover in Briggate by King Edward Street before proceeding to Lawnswood. *A. K. Terry*

Middle In Dewsbury Road, just beyond 'Tommy Wass's' public house in September 1953, 'Feltham' No 517, in the pleasing lined-out livery, is approaching the terminus before returning to Gipton on service No 11. As in so many of the other pictures, how quiet the scene is compared with today!

These cars were generally referred to by tram crews as 'London Cars', 'Feltham' being more commonly used when they worked in the Capital and also by enthusiasts. No 517 was one of four similar cars to receive an experimental 'diamond' pantograph in 1951. This was very short-lived as 517 disgraced herself one evening in City Square by fouling the overhead wires and pulling down a fair section, causing mayhem in the rush hour. The experiment was then deemed a failure and all four cars quickly reverted to bow collectors. Apparently, when 517's pantograph did the damage, the actual plate launched itself into the air and landed on the roof of the Majestic Cinema! It is said that the Manager handed the offending plate back to embarrassed Transport officials the following day! *A. K. Terry*

Bottom It's 2.10pm by the Corn Exchange clock on a fine, sunny afternoon in June 1955. 'Feltham' No 587 had left Kirkstall Road Works a short time ago after being refurbished, having spent five years in store. As can clearly be seen, it is in pristine condition and is making its way to Torre Road Depot before entering public service. 'The Whip' public house on the right is still there today (as indeed are all the buildings shown), though, as in many other shots, there has been a change of occupancy. *A. K. Terry*

THE CITY CENTRE

Above It's 5.55pm by the Guinness clock on 31 May 1957 at the Corn Exchange junction looking into Call Lane, and the rush hour is well under way, with two 'Feltham' cars passing in the evening sunshine. There is obviously some activity surrounding 505, with the conductress hanging resolutely on to the bow collector rope while the driver and inspector weigh up the situation. The answer to the cause of this hiatus can be found on page 86. The clock has now gone, replaced with a mural, as has the famous 'Hayes Oyster Bar' beneath it. Note the large barber's pole protruding from the Corn Exchange building, which at that time was also advertising Wallace Arnold coach tours. *A. K. Terry*

Above right A map of Leeds City Centre tramways in 1945, drawn by Bernard Donald. Changes by 1950 were that trams on Beckett Street were withdrawn in 1946; all inbound services were diverted from Marsh Lane in 1939, although the track remained usable for some time afterwards; and the West Street and St Paul's Street track was lifted after 1947 up to the crossover in Infirmary Street. *A. K. Terry*

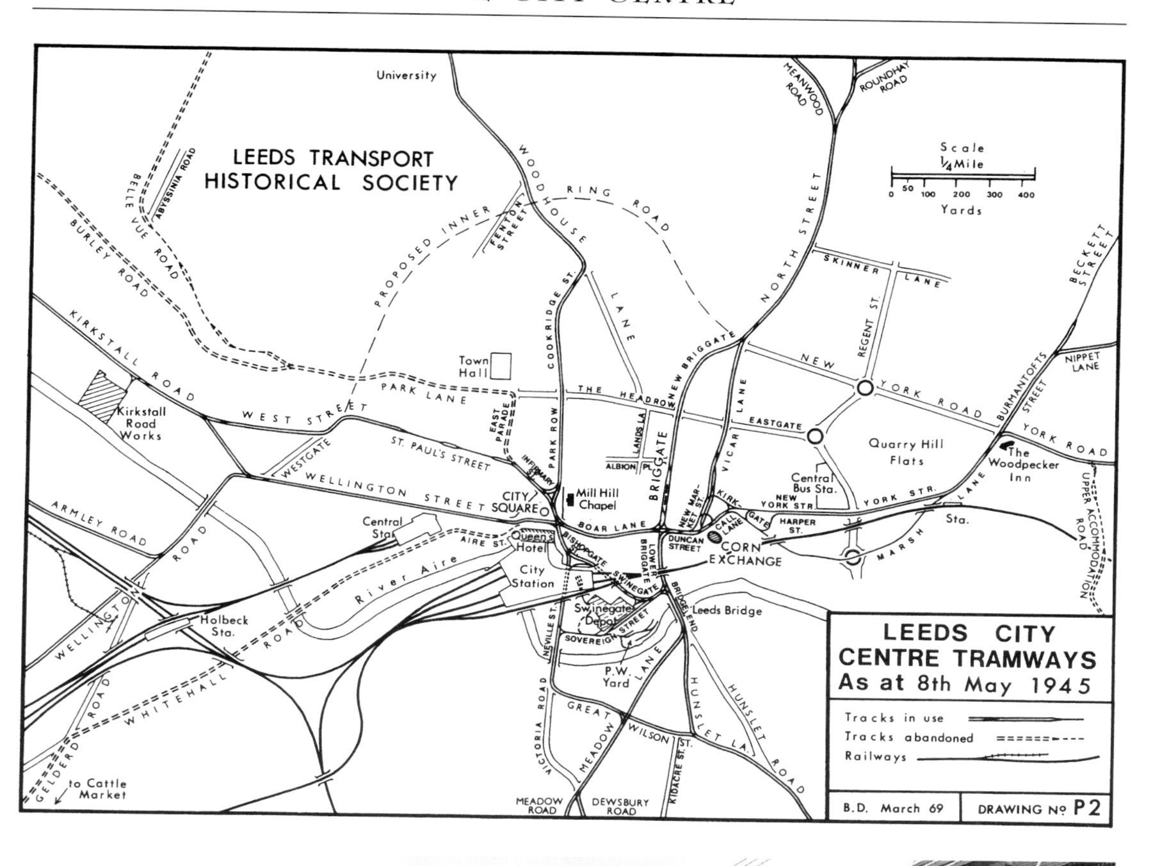

Right It is a very pleasant day, 25 May 1955, in North Street. Here, outside the Dispensary, the tram tracks were a good distance apart in the wide space afforded by the street. Many vehicles appear in the scene including a Standard 8, two Morris vans, a Wolseley and a Riley. Meanwhile, 'Feltham' No 505 pauses to pick up passengers bound for Harehills.

The tower with the clock in the background is that of Thomas Green & Son Ltd, founded in 1835, who, in earlier days, produced steam engines, locomotives, road-rollers, etc. In the 1950s they were particularly famous for lawnmowers and agricultural machinery. The building survives today in a restored state. Indeed, nearly all the property on this side of North Street survives. *A. K. Terry*

A splendid shot on 26 May 1955 a little further up North Street at the junction with Vicar Lane and New Briggate. 'Feltham' No 509 is on its way to the Crescent cinema, a short-working of service No 9. The Public Dispensary is in the left background and still stands today, although is now used for other purposes, while Arthur Cook's Furniture Showrooms and the property beyond the Dispensary are now all demolished. The Fordson lorry on the right belongs to Hey & Humphries – it's a long time since one could buy Heys Gold Cup Ale, the company having been taken over by Bass many years ago. *A. K. Terry*

The New York Street branch of the Yorkshire Penny Bank makes a perfect sandwich for two 'Feltham' cars, Nos 510 and 553. The bank was founded in 1859, the 'Penny' being dropped during the bank's centenary year in 1959. The Head Office has always been in Leeds, first at Infirmary Street and currently in Merrion Way, and the network covers most of the North and Midlands with some fairly recent encroachment into the South of England. The Yorkshire Bank is currently part of the National Bank of Australia, and this branch, which opened during the latter part of the 19th century, has now closed although the building survives.

In front of the Bank is a sharp curve, which the distant tram is about to negotiate; this enabled cars to turn back, usually for Temple Newsam. Note the louvred driver's windows in Nos 510 and 533; these were fine on warm, sunny days, but could be very draughty on cold, windy ones. Many were removed and replaced with one-piece windows. *A. K. Terry*

This is Wellington Street in May 1955, and 'Feltham' car No 543 is rumbling along on its way from Whingate to Cross Gates. Britannia House, which looks grubby at this time, is being let by Bramham & Gale: 'Office suites with passenger lift and central heating' are offered to would-be enquirers. It was, however, subsequently demolished and replaced by a modern building, St Martin's House.

Crowe & Co Ltd, as seen on the gable end on the left, was an old-established family business founded in 1857, dealing in wholesale clothing, soft furnishing, floor coverings and household drapery. The building, occupied by the company since 1904, still stands today. Note also in front of it the tiny 'West Yorkshire' bus station; this has now gone and a new building has been erected on the site. *A. K. Terry*

When the 'Feltham' cars were new into service they looked very smart indeed with their lined-out livery, and No 589 shows this to advantage, having just left Swinegate Depot and moving into Bridge End on its way to Parkside (at the bottom of Middleton Woods), once the home of Hunslet Rugby Club.

When the 'Felthams' ran in London, like most other trams they ran with trolleys in outer London and by a third-rail middle-conduit system in the central area. The rope holder for the trolley can clearly be seen on the cream band to the right of No 589's number. Despite all the cars using bow collectors while in Leeds, which also had a rope attached, the holders were never used.

Littlewoods are offering a jackpot prize of £75,000 at this time, 22 September 1956, which, if memory serves correctly, seemed to remain at this figure for many years. A bus crew just going on duty stare curiously at the camera, while Dawson's across the road want agents to form clubs. The faded writing on the wall suggests that a music shop existed here previously, offering repairs to accordions and saxophones. The corner property is now the 'Bridge Inn'. *A. K. Terry*

The Tong Road routes 15 and 16 hadn't long to go when this picture was taken on 6 July 1956. Already the queuing barriers in City Square have been taken down as 'Feltham' No 566 loads for New Inn, while the blackened Royal Exchange building proclaims the time to be 2.10pm. Demolition of this fine building was completed on 29 May 1964, and the replacement building has itself since been demolished, but the Mill Hill Chapel survives today as the only reminder of what was on that side of the square. Its wayside pulpit message of the day reads 'Judge not without knowledge nor without necessity and never without love'. Very profound. The penalty for dropping litter in 1956 was £5 – it seemed to work then, unlike today. *A. K. Terry*

A fairly peaceful scene in Kirkgate in September 1956. Much of the surroundings remain the same today although changes of ownership have taken place over the intervening years. 'Feltham' No 582 had not long been in service when this shot was taken, it being the very last car of the class to do so. It had been in store for almost six years and would only have a comparatively short life on the streets of Leeds before withdrawal and subsequent scrapping. *A. K. Terry*

This rare picture, taken on 4 July 1956, shows a tram on the track joining Swinegate with Bishopgate Street. 'Feltham' No 562 is showing 'Whingate' and is entering service from Swinegate Depot, which is unusual since, at that time, all services to Whingate and New Inn were worked solely from Torre Road Depot. The tram must have had a fault that had been rectified by fitters at Swinegate.

The queues at the two stops are for Hunslet (25) and Middleton (12). Behind them there is a newsagent's shop in the last arch before the girder bridge, which survives to this day. The poster on the wall is advertising *The Sporting Record*, with Harold King offering advice to punters on how to win on the Australian Pools. The large building in the background and the station canopy have long since gone, and today the vast bulk of 'City House' dominates the left background. Compare No 562 here with how it ended its days on page 87. *A. K. Terry*

Just to prove that the sun didn't always shine on the city during the 1950s, here is a very busy scene at the start of the rush hour on 17 July 1957: five trams and five buses fill the whole picture. By this time, of course, buses were becoming more and more in evidence as the tram services decreased.

Three 'Feltham' cars, Nos 574, 568 and 566 (which was lying defective), stand on Call Lane outside the Corn Exchange; the curve in the foreground was, by this time, out of use, but was originally the turning point for the No 14 service to Half Mile Lane, which last ran on 3 October 1953.

Samuel Smith's 'Star & Garter' public house closed in 1983 and the premises are currently let out as an amusement arcade. It is hoped to re-open the premises once more as a pub in the future. *A. K. Terry*

Above A heavy downpour has cleared and the sun has come out on this early May morning in 1955. It is hard to imagine that Wellington Street could ever have been so traffic-free when one thinks of today's volume. 'Feltham' No 558 is rumbling past the Great Northern Hotel and the entrance to Central Station. The hotel opened on 1 July 1869, but was badly damaged by fire on 27 July 1906 and subsequently rebuilt. It was, as the name suggests, built by the Great Northern Railway company and passed into LNER and later British Railways hands, only to be sold in 1952. It still stands today, but with a change of name to the Wellesley Hotel, thus giving it a connection with the street's name. The buildings in the background, except those in the far distance, remain much the same today, though cleaner and with changed occupancy. A Standard 8 is virtually the only other vehicle to be seen in what is today an extremely busy location. *A. K. Terry*

Above right On a cool September morning later in 1955, the 28th to be precise, another heavy downpour has cleared away as a fur-coated lady boards No 549 in Wellington Street. The building immediately above her had been occupied by the 'Walturdaw Cinema Supply Co', but had recently been acquired for G. Pick & Sons Ltd, well-known decorators' merchants of the day. The buildings occupied by W. Brayshay & Sons (see page 16) and the CWS still stand today but now serve other purposes.

The picture is so sharp that one feels one could walk out of Central Station today and observe the same scene, despite the fact that it was captured on film almost 50 years ago. It also shows up well the former London trams' distinctive features, including the bulbous driver's cab end. They were huge vehicles for their day, measuring some 40ft 10in from end to end. *A. K. Terry*

Right No 279 was one of three HR2 cars transferred from London in 1939, and the only one never to receive air-brakes. Drivers were instructed to stop the 18-ton vehicle with the hand-brake; the rheostatic/magnetic brake, which was used as common practice in the Capital, was only to be used in an emergency.

On 10 May 1954 we see a race around the corner from Briggate into Duncan Street, with the odds being heavily on the West Riding AEC Regent winning by a length on its way to Jumbles Lane. Is the conductor on No 279 giving the driver encouragement or merely telling him to release the hand-brake fully that they may go quicker?

The Fifty Shilling Tailors had originally been conceived as an idea by Sir Henry Price in 1928, whereby men could be provided with a suit incorporating the best of tailoring standards and value, all at a standard price of 50 shillings (£2.50). The business thrived, although after the war the title became something of a misnomer. Sir Henry retired in 1954 and was succeeded as Chairman by Mr John Collier and the Directors decided to adopt his as the trading name of the company. The rest, as they say, is history.

By the close of the 20th century the buildings stood blackened, empty and forlorn, awaiting redevelopment. Fortunately the facade, particularly that of the historic Dysons Time Ball Buildings complete with clock, were to be saved and incorporated in future developments. *A. K. Terry*

W. BRAYSHAY & SONS
WALTURDAW
CINEMA SUPPLY CO. LTD.
HALTON
20
MACKESON'S!
So strong—so smooth
549
BUS STOP
SERVICE
29 FARSLEY
30 BRADFORD
31 KEIGHLEY
YEADON
ILKLEY
QUEUE THIS SIDE

THE
FIFTY
SHILLING
TAILORS
LITTLEWOODS
EVERYONE LOOKS UP TO
LITTLEWOODS
SUPREME BY EVERY STANDARD
MEANWOOD
6
279
OF SOUND VALUE
AT YOUR CO-OPERATIVE STORE
14

One for the enthusiasts: a rare shot showing together all three types of former London trams that were transferred to Leeds between 1939 and 1951. An unidentified 'Feltham', HR2 No 278 and the unique No 301 are pictured passing the Transport Offices at the junction of Swinegate and Sovereign Street during the early evening of 12 June 1957. Around this location there was, as can plainly be seen, a veritable spider's web of overhead wires and trackwork, the entrance to the huge Swinegate Depot being just to the left of 301. You could, around this time, purchase a fireplace complete with the full works from Hardings across the street for £8 17s 6d. *A. K. Terry*

In Bridge End, at a point immediately over the River Aire, 'Middleton Bogie' car No 262 is about to turn left into Swinegate and return to Hunslet, Belle Isle and Middleton. 'Horsfield' No 226 in the background is going straight on up Briggate on its way to Gipton. Notice that there is not another vehicle in sight (except for the pram!) in what is now an extremely busy part of the city. On this particular day in March 1955, J. Crosswaite & Son are practising consultant medical herbalists – the premises, with the distinctive number 99 set into the wall, are now occupied by 'The Italian Job', a pizzeria. *A. K. Terry*

'Middleton Bogie' trams worked away from their own routes (Middleton and Hunslet) for a short time before they were scrapped. Here, on 22 June 1957, the last survivor, No 268, is crossing Kirkgate into New York Street on a Harehills Lane (17) service. What fine cars they were – such a great pity that none were preserved. The buildings remain much the same today, and although the 'Mason's Arms' behind No 268 is no more, the name and the Masonic symbols are still to be seen set into the wall. *A. K. Terry*

New Charles Roe-built railcar No 601 is taking one of her first journeys in service, on this occasion to New Inn, Wortley, in June 1953. This is City Square at Coronation time with the railway offices section of the City Station buildings in the background and the unique advertising obelisk of The News Theatre protruding above No 601's roof. This theatre opened on 22 June 1938, and had been variously known as the Tatler and Classic. It was originally provided to show short films for the benefit of people travelling and waiting for a connecting train or bus, but of course anyone could go in. Later it tried anything from feature length films to X-rated specials. In the 1990s, having been closed for some time, there were plans to re-open it on similar lines to the original.

The News Theatre was in the Queens Hotel complex. The first hotel opened on 10 January 1863 but was completely rebuilt in 1936-37 and stands today. Designed by W. Curtis Green and W. Hamlyn, who, at the time, were asked to carry out a design to a 'Cosmopolitan classic with a decided transatlantic bias', it was not enthusiastically received by the public when it opened. *A. K. Terry*

Above On a glorious sunny day 'Horsfield' car No 238 swings round from Duncan Street into Briggate on service No 5 to Beeston – observe the conductor's hand-signal. It is 28 July 1955, exactly 92 years to the day since the Corn Exchange opened. Three outfitters can be seen next door to each other – Reid Bros, Alexandre and Rawcliffe's; Burton's is also on the corner (where the Briggate sign is). Only Rawcliffe's survive in the same spot today. *A. K. Terry*

Above right n May 1952 a very labour-intensive scene occupies Duncan Street at 11.10am. Track replacement is taking place, which has caused 'Horsfield' car No 165 to pause before proceeding gingerly over the workings on its way to Elland Road.

The blackened 'tiers' of Holy Trinity Church dominate the background. The foundation stone was laid in 1722 and the building was opened (having cost £5,463 12s 5d) five years later in 1727. The present 'spire' was only added in 1839. *A. K. Terry*

Right Little of the general scenery at this location has changed today; the buildings remain much the same, although some modern development has taken place in the background of this July 1991 photograph. Burton's became an Oxfam shop and Samuel Smith's 'Central Market Hotel' is now called 'The Hollywood'. This establishment has had something of a chequered career since this shot was taken. It changed its name in 1969 to 'The Admiral'; ten years later it changed again, this time to 'Barbarellas', then in 1981 it changed yet again to become known as 'Hollywood Days and Nights'. Sam Smith's sold the pub to Websters in 1986. *F. Whiley*

WATSON
BOOTH'S
SAMUEL SMITH
BURTON
165

SOMETHING SPECIAL
Station
Infirmary
University
HAIR

FRANKS
YORK
SELBY
HULL
HEADINGLEY
1
Beer at its Best!
211
H. SAMUEL

2
CIRCULAR
MOORTOWN
LITTLEWOODS
196
FRED VERITY & SON
DYSONS

Left A marked lack of other vehicular traffic is the striking feature of this midday scene on 25 June 1953 looking up Briggate towards the loading barriers. 'Horsfield' car No 211 waits at the lights together with a Standard Vanguard, before swinging into Boar Lane en route for Headingley.

Although the clothing trade was the prime industry that made Leeds famous (note The Fifty Shilling Tailors next door to H. Samuel), one other notable institution is featured in the picture, and which has been synonymous with the city for many years – Tetleys. It all really began on 31 October 1822, when Joshua Tetley, then the head of an established family of maltsters based in Armley, struck a deal to buy a brewery in Salem Place, Hunslet, from one William Sykes. The business, after a shaky start, grew rapidly with many sales outlets being opened. The first public house bought by Joshua Tetley & Son, in 1890, was 'The Duke William', which still stands today in the brewery yard. Many take-overs have taken place over the years to make Tetleys, in association with Ind Coope and Ansells (now part of Allied Lyons), one of the best-known names in the brewing trade. *A. K. Terry*

Below left 'Horsfield' car No 196 rattles over the junction at Bridge End into Briggate giving a good example of how one used to be able to leap on and off open-platform vehicles so easily. The tram is on its way from Dewsbury Road to Moortown on the 2 Circular via Chapeltown.

Fred Verity's shop on the right was a well-known ironmongers for many years before finally ceasing trading some little while ago. The Jowett/Bradford van is about to turn into Swinegate. At this time, 27 April 1957, these were common vehicles and were quite remarkable with their four-stroke two-cylinder engines. Jowett's also produced the 'Javelin' car, a superb vehicle probably years ahead of its time. I suspect few of either van or car exist today. *A. K. Terry*

Below An animated scene in New Market Street on 4 October 1953. The previous evening, services to Half Mile Lane and Bramley were withdrawn and with them the special curve at the Corn Exchange where they loaded. Overnight, the triple track in New Market Street was altered to allow trams to Beeston and Elland Road to take an easier course to their loading barriers. This involved laying a zig-zag curve, and here, in the brightness of Sunday lunchtime, car No 255 carefully traverses the new curve to load for Elland Road. A genuine steam-roller completes the scene.

The surroundings are very much the same today. Shop ownership has, inevitably, changed, with the much-loved Maypole Dairy now a Barratt's shoe shop and Benefit Footwear now part of Curtess shoes. *A. K. Terry*

12
MIDDLETON
Step out in Stylo FASHION SHOES
180
WOODWORKERS Supply Stores
WOODWORKERS Supply Stores
PELMETS
PELMETS

TUNSTALL & CO. LTD
DAMP COURSES
ROOF FELTS
BITUMEN & TARVARNISH
WOOD & IRON PRESERVATIVES
TUNSTALL & Co LTD ESTD 1835
26
BALM ROAD
Step out in Stylo FASHION SHOES
Player's Please
166
TRAM STOP
Wm YOUNGER'S MONK EXPORT
Milk can do so much for you!
ALL CATS
COOKED AND R

Above left At Kirkgate tram stop near the city markets on 2 September 1957, a cheerful, whistling driver awaits the bell before moving off on a 'straight' Middleton, as against the car behind on a 'Circular'. 'Horsfield' car No 180 was later saved from the scrapyard and moved to the National Tramway Museum at Crich.

Woodworkers Supply Stores was a wonderful source of excellent timber and woodworking tools until, like so many businesses, it succumbed to one of the seemingly endless post-war recessions. It will be noted that pelmets were still very much in vogue.

Two pedestrians look askance at the photographer standing in the middle of the street taking a snap of what was still then an everyday object. It is, however, fortunate that such people existed to record the passage of history. *A. K. Terry*

Left This fine, solid building remains to this day. Tunstall & Co Ltd, established 1835, has long since gone, but today the much cleaned building houses the Good Impressions printing company.

It is the early evening of Friday 31 August 1956 in Hunslet Lane at the corner of Waterloo Street. 'Horsfield' car No 166 is on a rare short-working to Balm Road and is running on track that was closed to regular service trams (although remaining serviceable) before the Second World War until the creation of the new through services between York Road and south Leeds in 1956.

The small adverts on the hoardings tell us that Odsal Stadium has just hosted the final meeting of the season between themselves and Norwich, while Chris Barber's Jazz Band with Ottilie Patterson is to appear at the Town Hall on the coming Sunday accompanied by the Dick Bishop Skiffle Group, for goodness sake! *A. K. Terry*

Above This is the unmistakable location of City Square on a dull August day in 1954. 'Horsfield' car No 216 is about to enter Boar Lane on its way to Moortown on the 2 Circular service. Trams for Headingley and Lawnswood last ran through City Square on 3 March 1956.

The fine Norwich Union Building in the right background was demolished in the 1960s and replaced with a soulless glass box – truly a planning tragedy. It is ironic that the replacement building became due for demolition itself. A few yards from this spot lies City Station where, in 1956, you could have gone on a day excursion to Blackpool for 9s 9d (48p) during the week, or the extortionate price of 12s 6d on a Saturday! *A. K. Terry*

No, the conductor isn't trying to hang himself! Cars from York Road, other than those from Temple Newsam, usually reversed in Duncan Street if they had only worked into the city. With centre poles still used, it was necessary to reverse the bow collector on the high wire on the crossover itself. This was quite a manoeuvre and required some strength, hence the conductor using the tram's fender to gain extra purchase. His 'Chamberlain' car, No 139, is about to return to Harehills Lane on the No 17.

The blackened Corn Exchange dominates the background. Built between 1861 and 1863 it cost, including the site, £32,415, a considerable amount of money then. Its original purpose as an exchange has now ceased; the building has been cleaned and houses modern shops and similar retail facilities.

Older readers who can remember the late, great comedian Albert Modley may notice that the bus on the right-hand side is going to 'Duplicate'. Albert used to incorporate this into one of his stage sketches using a drum kit as a pretend tram controller. *A. K. Terry*

A rather weary and well-worn 'Chamberlain' car, No 1, makes its way along New York Street past the Central bus station. The queue of people at the stop seem to have little chance of boarding as No 1 appears to be well filled on its way to Temple Newsam.

Observe the extra use made of the span wire supporting the overhead cable. It was common around this time, and I suppose had been for many years, to suspend street lights from the wires, thus saving the expense of having to erect a separate lamp-post. *A. K. Terry*

INNER SUBURBS

The three most popular trams in Leeds must have been the 'Lance Corporals' (nicknamed for obvious reasons), Nos 272, 273 and 274, built at Kirkstall Road Works in 1934-35. They were intended to work primarily on the smart residential routes to Headingley, Moortown and Roundhay, and were originally painted in a lavish pale blue and cream. With their special very deep cushioned seating, which had to be swivelled/rotated (as opposed to turned over) at each terminus, and, at the time, a driver's seat also, they were very well liked by both passengers and crews.

In later years they were painted in the red and cream livery and their headlamps were recessed (as seen here) to minimise accidental damage. Even their high-backed seats had to be replaced by more conventional turn-over ones when the new Ultimate ticket machines arrived. From an essentially Leeds point of view, it is something of a tragedy that one of these luxurious trams was never saved for preservation; all were withdrawn and broken up at the end of 1955. Here we see No 273 in Woodhouse Lane outside the University in September 1954. *A. K. Terry*

Above A typical scene in North Street on a fine, warm day, 19 July 1958. The splendid array of shops on the right has now all gone, and pedestrian traffic is much lighter than it was in the 1950s. Note the small boys on the right with their shorts, braces and 'pumps'. The hoarding on the wall on the extreme left is advertising Premium Bonds, which, when this photograph was taken, had been on sale for just over one and a half years. The jackpot prize then was £1,000 – quite a sum. The top prize today is £1,000,000 – you could have bought quite a bit of property on North Street for that in 1958!

'Horsfield' No 178 has just passed Grafton Street and is followed by a Bedford Duple coach, fine vehicles that typify the period and were then a common sight; quite a few survive today as preserved vehicles. No 178 was one of two specially illuminated cars that took part in the final procession, the other being No 160. *A. K. Terry*

Above right After the trams finished, North Street was soon developed into a one-way street in the out-of-city direction. All the property on the left (in tramway days mostly occupied by Jewish tailors) has long since gone. On the 'beer and fags' corner of Wintoun Street is Cohen's shop, which appears to sell everything from newspapers to vegetables! 'Irn-Bru' also stands out well – still very popular, although I suspect it was then more of a Scottish drink than its more universal appeal today.

Below the Capstan hoarding the Majestic Cinema is advertising *Dracula*, which is described in *Halliwell's Film Guide* as: 'A "Hammer" remake of the 1930 film. Commendably brief in comparison with later Hammer films. This was perhaps the best horror piece they turned out as well as the most faithful to its original. Decor and colour were well used and the leading performances are striking.' The film's two great stars were Peter Cushing and Christopher Lee. The Majestic opened on 5 June 1922 and closed with a performance of *The Good, the Bad and the Ugly* on 10 July 1969 to become a bingo establishment. By the time this picture was taken, on 19 July 1958, only trams from Roundhay still worked along the street, with No 202 seen here leading a line of traffic. *A. K. Terry*

Right Looking at the same view more than 30 years later it is almost inconceivable that North Street could ever have looked as it did in tram days. On a dismal 15 July 1991, at a fairly quiet time for traffic, only the old Midland Bank building at 'Golden Cross' remains as a reminder of just how things were. *F. Whiley*

Barr's
IRN-BRU
The Perfect
Mineral Water
CAPSTAN
take the strain
BEER ½
the best long drink
in the world!
WINTOUN STREET
GALES
BRIGGATE
202
LCK 290

Halifax A58
M'ways
(M621,M62)
Meanwood Sheepscar
Harrogate A61 Wetherby A58
Chapeltown Harehills

Above A closer view of the point known locally as 'Golden Cross' junction after the public house that can be seen to the left. 'Horsfield' car No 224 has left the 'main line' and has entered Meanwood Road on service No 6. The Midland Bank on the right last opened for business in November 1978. As seen on the previous page, this is now an extremely busy junction of the Sheepscar gyratory road system, the 'Golden Cross' having been demolished at the time of road construction. *A. K. Terry*

Above right The library at Sheepscar always helped to identify photographs. A library first opened here in 1877, but the present building dates from 1938. It closed as a library on 4 June 1976, although the premises remain today as the Leeds District Archives. Chapeltown Branch Post Office adjoined the library on the left and again is still there today, though no longer a post office, having closed for business in December 1985.

When this picture was taken in August 1956 it was not uncommon to see three or four trams moving to and fro. The tracks to the left lead to Moortown via Chapeltown and those to the right to Roundhay via Harehills. *A. K. Terry*

Right On 15 July 1991 the old library building and post office stand in splendid isolation, although 'The Victoria' on the right still keeps them company. *F. Whiley*

SHEEPSCAR
TIZER
LIBRARY

SHEEPSCAR

Above In July 1952, a quiet scene sees 'Feltham' car No 534 (still bearing scars of its former days in London) about to turn into Marsh Lane. The splendid London & North Eastern Railway grain warehouse was, unfortunately, subsequently ravaged by fire and demolished. *A. K. Terry*

Below This scene would surely have appealed to the late, great Lawrence Stephen Lowry himself. 'Horsfield' car No 225 heads off down Nippet Lane on her way to Compton Road terminus. Service 10 closed in April 1954. Looking at the picture one forgets just how dark the streets were at night, lit only by gas lamps. Today anyone returning to this scene in a time-warp would think they were in the wartime blackout! The smoking chimneys in the background were part of the Burmantofts brickworks renowned for its 'beautiful, architectural terra-cotta bricks'. Preliminary work has already been carried out to prepare for the new trams to cross the road here. *R. Wiseman*

Above Truly a further scene from another world! This is Stoney Rock Lane at the junction of Fraser Street, with 'Chamberlain' car No 124 descending the incline on its way to Dewsbury Road on route 9. Just look how many corner shops there are! No having to trail to the supermarket in those days – almost everything was to hand.

A tram driver once described this portion of route 9 as 'like driving up and down a ruddy snake's back!' such was its endless twists and turns. There seemed to be bends in the track even where there were no bends in the road! *R. Wiseman*

Below This is the junction of Burmantofts Street, Beckett Street and Nippet Lane – barely recognisable today. The truncated trackwork to the left is all that remains of the service to Harehills via Beckett Street, which last ran on 24 August 1946. On this day in June 1953 'Feltham' car No 513 is making its way on service No 9 to Compton Road, although the screen has already been changed for the return journey to Dewsbury Road. This was a busy service, patronised particularly at peak times by employees of the huge Burton factory in Hudson Road. The mills complex had been started in 1920 and was gradually added to until the final section was completed in the mid-1930s; in October 1934 the then Princess Royal opened the new canteen, which accommodated 8,000 employees (at one sitting!) and where, according to the Leeds Mercury, 'one could have a mid-day meal of meat, potatoes, vegetables, bread and pudding for 10d'!

Burton's has changed somewhat over the ensuing years, particularly after the decline of the 'made-to-measure' market in men's outerwear. The group duly adapted and diversified in a major way, opening 'new' fashion outlets like 'Top Shop', 'Principles' and 'Champion Sport'. With Burton's once again in a dominant position, there can be little doubt that Sir Montague, who died in 1952, would be delighted. *A. K. Terry*

HYDE PARK
27
513
CKY 751

MIDDLETON
12 CIRCULAR
Best of All! SUNSHINE BREAD Best of All!
BAKERS JESSE STEPHENSON LTD FARSLEY
590
SOCIETY
REFUGE LENDING SOCIETY LTD.
ENTRANCE

Above left In Great Wilson Street in June 1955 a little 'soft top' Standard 8 is parked alongside 'Feltham' No 513 as it unloads at the 'Part-day, Monday-Friday only' service 27 tram stop to Hyde Park. In the background a 'Middleton Bogie' car is crossing 'Christ Church' junction on its way from Middleton to Swinegate.

All this scenery has now been swept away to make room for the gyratory road systems leading to the M1 and M621. Note the hand signal from the British Road Services lorry driver on the left. *A. K. Terry*

Left Another backcloth that has totally disappeared. 'Feltham' No 590 (the last of these cars to leave London, on 3 October 1951) turns from Great Wilson Street into Meadow Lane to work the 12 Circular to Middleton. At the same spot today the roads have been dramatically widened and, behind where the tram is pictured on 19 July 1956, Asda Foods has built a new headquarters complex. Note the Sunbeam Talbot and three-wheel Bond mini-car in the background. *A. K. Terry*

Above The day before service No 6 from Elland Road to Meanwood would finish, 24 June 1955, 'Feltham' No 513, in excellent external condition, thunders over 'Christ Church' junction in Meadow Lane. Wildblood & Ward, Printers and Stationers (to the right of No 513), was an old-established family firm, sadly no longer in existence. The Guinness advert, featuring the famous toucans, shows up well in this scene, which has completely changed today. *A. K. Terry*

Above A truly classic early/mid-1950s scene, with blackened buildings and the ubiquitous corner shop, which appears to be a Post Office (New Wortley?)-cum-greengrocers. With the nowadays extremely rare gas-holder dominating the background, you can almost smell the atmosphere!

Here we are on Wellington Road at the junction of Campbell Street, with 'Feltham' car No 533 heading for New Inn on a fine sunny day. Virtually the whole of this area is now but a memory and is part of the Armley gyratory interchange. *R. Wiseman*

Below This is the junction at the west end of Wellington Street where the former Kirkstall and Guiseley routes diverged to the right from those to Bramley, Stanningley, Pudsey and Wortley. 'Feltham' No 587 is heading for New Inn with the Kirkstall junction still intact, despite the fact that the last service car had used it on 3 April 1954; the tracks were still needed for access to Kirkstall Road Works. which eventually closed on 7 November 1957. No 587, seen here in August 1955, had not long entered service (see also page 79), having been stored for almost five years.

Almost all this scene disappeared many years ago under a flyover that formed part of the new inner ring road. Yorkshire Evening Post newspapers developed property on the right at this point, while the remainder of the street running up to City Square has always been somewhat haphazardly developed, being, as it is, on the fringe of the City Centre. The area suffered some bomb damage during the last war when the enemy targeted the bridge over the river, the canal and the railway yards in Wellington Road, and has not altogether recovered today.

At the Grand Theatre, Jane Hylton and Derek Bond are appearing in a play entitled *Men and Women*. The Grand opened on 18 November 1878 and was nearly demolished in 1969, being saved by the intervention of the City Council; it survives to this day. *A. K. Terry*

Above Tong Road in west Leeds provided typical working-class rows of back-to-back houses, intensive living and well-used public transport. The trams on the services to Whingate and New Inn were frequent right up until the last one ran on 21 July 1956. Here, on 17 August 1955, 'Feltham' No 564 passes hand-braked 'Chamberlain' No 112 at Fifteenth Avenue – since demolished.

In addition to 'hairdressing to suit individual tastes' at Max's on the corner, you could also buy Turf and Robin cigarettes – remember them? One wonders what Max would make of today's modern, flamboyant hairstyles! *A. K. Terry*

Below This is Tong Road at the junction of Strawberry Lane on Sunday 4 April 1954, and 'Feltham' car No 549 slips past the Leeds Industrial Co-operative Society, which, of course, in those days sold a large variety of items all under the one roof. Although the Co-op has long since vacated the premises, the building (something of an architectural gem) survives to this day.

The many adverts on the newsagent's wall on the left range from 'Murderers Fought in Cell' in the *Weekly News* and Ava Gardner's secretary 'Tells All' in *Glamour* magazine to *Sunny Stories* (I remember it well) – 'Happy, wholesome reading for the younger child'. I suspect today's younger generation would view the publication with utter contempt.

The hand-pulled electric milk-float on the left was a familiar sight at this time and for many years afterwards, and was synonymous with the seemingly more relaxed and less stressful nature of days gone by. *R. Wiseman*

Above Soon after entering Wellington Road, trams to New Inn and Whingate crossed the railway track connecting the two halves of the local gas works. Here we see a wonderfully 'posed' shot of a Ruston & Hornsby diesel locomotive crossing over and holding up oncoming traffic. Generally speaking, locos would only cross when traffic was light and certainly not when a tram was coming. On 8 May 1956, when this scene was enacted, service 15 to Whingate had but a few weeks of life left and No 559 would find work on other services.

'Appleyard for Morris' proclaims the advert on the bridge, a well-known name at the time. They were distributors of Morris, Wolseley, Riley and MG cars, and dealers for Austin, as well as many other activities, and extended around Leeds, Huddersfield, Bradford and Harrogate. The company claimed to have the largest garage area – more than 5 acres – in Europe, with, at the end of the 1950s, a staff of well over 600. *A. K. Terry*

Below The backdrop to this scene in Wellington Road disappeared long ago when the new inner ring road was built, skirting the new property of the *Yorkshire Evening Post.* However, on 2 October 1954 things look as if they would remain for ever, as 'Feltham' No 553 attacks the incline en route to New Inn, while a motorcycle combination (with rider and passenger sans helmets) passes by. The large adverts pasted on the wall speak for themselves – the small ones advertise a variety of items from a 'Battle of the Roses' Speedway meeting at Odsal Stadium to a special Bible address in the City Mission on Park Row. The Theatre Royal is advertising the Court Players in four productions, the three identifiable ones being *Birthday Honours*, *On Probation* and *Dial 'M' for Murder*. The Theatre Royal opened in October 1876, and I suppose its great claim to fame was its association with the pantomime and all its traditions. The great impresario Francis Laidler will long be remembered with affection for all the productions he undertook. Sadly the theatre finally closed on 30 March 1957 and was subsequently demolished. *A. K. Terry*

OUTER SUBURBS AND BEYOND

In Chapeltown Road, on a fine summer evening, 16 July 1956, the classic lines of 'Horsfield' car No 246 show up well as the car crosses over at Reginald Terrace on a rare short-working back to Briggate. *A. K. Terry*

Parkinson's
BISCUITS

9
TIZER
TIZER
124

Above left In the lower part of Chapeltown Road, outside St Clement's Church, much of the backcloth to this scene has changed today out of all recognition. The church and many other nearby properties were demolished in the 1960s to make room for part of the new Sheepscar interchange junction. Most of the buildings were Victorian, but even today occasional examples survive in isolation amid an almost continuous flurry of passing traffic. Here, on 8 July 1955, 'Chamberlain' car No 142 heads for Lawnswood with remarkably little traffic accompanying it. *A. K. Terry*

Left Here is proof, if proof were needed, that Leeds was not all back-to-back housing and industry. This is the terminus at Moortown corner on 9 July 1955, where cars on the two Circular routes (No 2 via Chapeltown and No 3 via Harehills) would meet and 'lay over' for a while before both of them returned to the city. 'Horsfield' car No 169 is working a No 1 service back to Lawnswood, while 'Chamberlain' car No 124, freshly painted in red and cream, has just reversed, having arrived via Chapeltown as a 'straight' No 2 to Moortown before returning to Dewsbury Road on service No 9. 'Tizer the Appetizer' was a frequent advert seen on the front dash end of trams and, of course, is still as popular today. *A. K. Terry*

Above Here is a quintessential 1950s scene in high summer, on Saturday 6 July 1957 at Moortown corner. The first Saturday in July was always 'Children's Day' at Roundhay Park – sports, galas, etc for Leeds schools. This point was both a terminus and a 'lay-over' for trams on one of the circular routes.

'Showboat' car No 205 carries an advert for 'Spot Garages', a famous name in the motor trade in earlier days. It is said that when Mr G. Abbott began his business in 1930, his first premises in Grove Lane were so small that he was diffident about incorporating the word 'garage' in his trading name; he therefore decided to call it 'The Spot for Repairs'. It became a limited company in 1947 and was at one time reputed to carry one of the largest stocks of tyres in Leeds, also claiming, among other things, to undertake 'invisible' body repairs! *A. K. Terry*

Above In the almost sylvan setting of Street Lane, midway between Moortown and Roundhay, on 10 July 1955, 'Horsfield' No 181 has worked a 3 Circular route via Roundhay, and the conductor has already reset the indicator to return, via Chapeltown, to Lawnswood. No 181 held the distinction of being the last tram in public service on 7 November 1959 before the official procession took to the streets. The tram apart, little has changed here today. *A. K. Terry*

Above right A fine, crisp late winter's day, 28 March 1959 was a significant date in Leeds tramway history, for it was to be not only the final day that trams would work north of the city to Moortown, but also the wonderful Middleton and Belle Isle routes were to close. The system was now all but dead – only the York Road routes (and the No 25 route to Hunslet for a further three weeks) were left the following day to soldier on through the long hot summer to come.

We see here 'Horsfield' No 158 trundling along Street Lane near Moortown. Little has changed here over the intervening years save for the considerable increase in traffic. Notice the fading white bands on the trees, a relic from the blackout of the Second World War. *A. K. Terry*

Right At the unmistakable location of Roundhay Park main entrance on Sunday afternoon, 22 April 1951, 'Chamberlain' car No 72, in its special red livery with narrow lower cream band, pauses to load before heading towards the city. It has a 'three-blind' indicator, soon to be phased out – the very lowest part (or 'via' screen) would be blanked off. These cars were commonly referred to as 'Pushers' by tram crews because drivers had to push on the handbrake to stop them.

Melbourne Ales was a well-known brew around the city for many years, with its distinctive 'courtier' symbol and familiar bright red lorries making frequent deliveries. The company's history goes back to 1840, when Dickinson & Co began brewing in Plum Street, Leeds; it subsequently greatly expanded, taking over other small breweries as time passed. However, Melbourne Brewery Ltd was itself to be taken over by the mighty Tetley on 1 April 1960.

Note the little girl on the three-wheel bike with father on the other end of the 'lead'. *A. K. Terry*

BRIGGATE
Step out in Stylo FASHION SHOES
158

3
CIRCULAR ROUTE
BRIGGATE
MELBOURN
ALES
CAPSTAN
TRAMWAY
FARE STAGE
72

MOORTOWN
3
198

HOVIS
RKINS
MIDLAND BANK LIMITED
LLOYDS BANK LIMITED
C. Webdale BUILDER
GWT 670
265
RNW 331

Left This bucolic scene in Prince's Avenue, between Oakwood and Roundhay, on a very pleasant afternoon in May 1958, reminds us that even in a heavily built-up industrial city like Leeds, there are always pockets of green open space like this to give a complete contrast. *A. K. Terry*

Below left In Roundhay Road, at the junction of Harehills Road, on 12 May 1956, the tracks on the right are the remnants of the former Harehills Road via Beckett Street route, which was discontinued in 1946; however, these terminal tracks were still in occasional use for Bank Holiday and Sunday extras to and from Roundhay Park.

The scene is unique in having a 'Middleton Bogie' car, No 265, passing on its way to Easterly Road, Harehills. Only on this one Saturday was this tram allocated to work duties on routes Nos 2, 3 and 9, and it was duly photographed by more than one enthusiast! The Ford Prefect on the right is in excellent condition and very reminiscent of the times. *A. K. Terry*

Below Even though this is a Sunday morning, how amazingly quiet the scene is compared with today! At the junction of Roundhay Road and Easterly Road at the Clock Cinema on 10 July 1955, 'Horsfield' car No 166 is en route for Headingley on service No 1, having come round on Circular route 2 via Moortown. The lines branching off to the left merely ended in a spur for cars terminating here. The single-deck, centre-entrance bus turning from Harehills Lane into Roundhay Road will terminate there before returning on the long suburban 45 route to Wortley.

The Harehills Parade branch of the Yorkshire Penny Bank opened on 6 July 1936, and the art deco building survives today as an Asian dress shop. An Armstrong Siddeley car in the foreground completes the scene. *A. K. Terry*

Below A further view of the Clock Cinema, Harehills, looking in the opposite direction. On 29 September 1956 some track replacement is taking place at the junction of Easterly Road, and *Reach for the Sky* is the main attraction. There is a queue to get in, and a sign stating '2nd House Fully Booked'. *Halliwell's Film Guide* describes *Reach for the Sky* as a 'box office exploitation of Douglas Bader's personal heroism, adequately but not inspiringly put together with many stiff upper lips and much jocular humour.' The film starred Kenneth More and Muriel Pavlow. The Clock opened on 12 November 1938 and showed its last film on 28 February 1976, after which it became the inevitable Bingo Hall. Even this came to an end and today the building, which is listed, is an electrical store.

Car 276, shown here, was a 'one-off' built by the Transport Department in 1948. It was to be the forerunner of a class of 50 but, for various reasons, no more were constructed. It survived until October 1957. *A. K. Terry*

Right When the Harehills Road via Beckett Street service finished on 24 August 1946, the junction at its terminus with Roundhay Road, together with the terminal crossover, was left in situ. This enabled trams to be worked at busy times between Roundhay Park and Harehills Road, and at other times to store the occasional defective car out of the way.

This scene, taken on 2 August 1952 and looking towards Roundhay Road, shows 'Feltham' car No 517 on one of these special workings. The AEC Regent bus on the right, taking over part of the 42 route (which replaced both the Beckett Street and Lower Wortley routes as a new through service) is working only between Harehills and Eastgate as a Sunday afternoon special to carry visitors to and from St James's Hospital.

Note the 'H'-shaped television aerial on the chimney stack immediately above the bus roof. It stands on its own, but is very much a sign of things to come! *A. K. Terry*

Below right The short extension to Gipton Estate was only laid in 1936 and was about a quarter of a mile long, branching off from York Road. It was originally intended to be just the start of a much longer extension to Seacroft; in fact, at some time during the 1940s 'Seacroft' was inserted (along with Belle Isle) on the destination screen. Here at the terminus cars 34 and 215 pass each other. Had the extension materialised, the line seen here would have continued across Wykebeck Valley Road on a side reservation, crossing Foundry Lane, along what became South Parkway Approach, into South Parkway and past Ironwood View to a terminus at Seacroft Hall, York Road. Two other extensions were also planned into Seacroft, one as an extension from Compton Road via Oak Tree Drive and the other from the Melbourne Hotel to Barwick Road. None of them came about for a variety of reasons, and one can only guess what effect these imaginative plans would have had on the tramway system. *A. K. Terry*

3
517

9
CROSS FLATTS
mens wear
JOHN
WARREN
79 VICAR LANE
34
DEWSBURY RD
9
MELBOURNE
ALES
215

Above The 'Middleton Bogie' cars rarely worked regularly other than to Middleton and Hunslet until after the closure of the Tong Road services to Whingate and New Inn in 1956. Thereafter the York Road services to Cross Gates, Halton and Temple Newsam were joined with Middleton and Belle Isle. The few bogie cars left in service then spent the short time remaining of their lives working both in south Leeds and along York Road, the latter for the first time. None of them survived to see the end of the system in 1959.

Quite often one or two could be seen working on the Corn Exchange-Temple Newsam (22) service for which they would have been very well suited if the schedule had not been so relaxed. This picture, taken on 8 September 1956, shows car No 257 at Plantation Avenue on its way down from Halton to Temple Newsam. *A. K. Terry*

Above right 'Horsfield' car No 203 leans into the curve away from the public highway on the lower part of Temple Newsam Road. Although busy in summer, winter traffic was sparse and the half-hourly service often ran empty. *A. K. Terry*

Right 'Feltham' No 550 is at rest in the positively sylvan setting of Temple Newsam tram terminus in July 1952. Not long into service, it has still not received its side panel advert. *A. K. Terry*

22
TEMPLENEWSAM
TETLEYS
Beer at its Best!
203

EXCHANGE
550

BALM ROAD
26
SIGN OF SOUND VALUE AT YOUR CO-OPERATIVE STORE
301

SWINEGATE
259
Player's Please

Above left It's a fine, sunny evening on 14 June 1957 as car No 301 swings into Balm Road from Church Street, Hunslet. No 301 made very occasional journeys to Balm Road, which was a short-working of the Belle Isle route.

This car was from London, sent in place of two 'Felthams' that had been burned out while in the Capital. Numbered 1 while there, she arrived in Leeds in December 1951 and was renumbered 301. A truly superb vehicle with clean lines and good all-round top-deck vision, fortunately she survives today at the National Tramway Museum at Crich in Derbyshire.

The new trams will soon be turning this corner at almost the same location. *A. K. Terry*

Left 'Middleton Bogie' car No 259 turns from Balm Road into Church Street on its way to Swinegate in September 1954. The steel pieces that can be seen welded to the tram's fenders were to prevent damage by over-riding from other trams. Whether this worked or not is a matter of conjecture. *A. K. Terry*

Above On the Elland Road route, 'Horsfield' car No 239 is loading at Lane End Place at the bottom of Holbeck Moor before returning to Meanwood. Everything in this scene, including the splendid Vauxhall 10, is now completely gone to make way for the M621 motorway. It is 25 June 1955, the last day that service No 6 would run. *A. K. Terry*

BEER
BYB
NEW PEACOCK INN
SPECIAL CAR
246

Scott's Porage
BUTLER'S
BUTLER'S
WOODBINES
CRAVEN 'A'
SPECIAL CAR
199
SALT

Above left This scene is unique. The Elland Road route had been left intact after the service was replaced by buses on 25 June 1955 in order to retain access to the scrapyard in Low Fields Road. With the fuel shortages resulting from the Suez Crisis in 1956 and early 1957, it was decided to allow some trams to operate again to Low Fields Road siding to supplement the football bus specials. The day before this commenced, 8 December 1956, 'Horsfield' car No 246 was sent on a test journey from Swinegate Depot and is seen here arriving near the football ground followed by a tower wagon.

No 246 was one of the cars used the following day to carry passengers along the route. The special service continued until 16 March 1957 when, with the easier availability of fuel, the buses could take over again. Trams continued to go to the scrapyard on a one-way journey during the night for only a short time longer. *A. K. Terry*

Left Here is a scene during that period. It is a wet Saturday in January 1957 and Leeds United are at home to Cardiff City in the Third Round of the FA Cup. The final result made the day seem even gloomier – Leeds lost 1-2, Charles scoring for the home side in front of a crowd of 34,237.

'Horsfields' Nos 199 and 254 (the last-numbered in the class), at Hoxton Mount crossover, prepare to return to the City Centre to pick up more would-be supporters. Note the two policemen on the motorcycle – no crash helmets required in those days. *A. K. Terry*

Above This is the service terminus outside Leeds United Football Club ground in Elland Road on 18 June 1955, just seven days before the trams would be replaced by buses. 'Horsfield' cars Nos 208 and 156 pass each other – 208 is returning to Meanwood, incorrectly showing the pre-war 23 service number instead of the usual 6. Apart from the Guinness and Mackeson adverts, there is also one for Anglo XL chewing gum – I can't remember seeing that for a long time. *A. K. Terry*

Above Well over a year before the Suez Crisis blew up, this was a common sight to gladden the heart of any tram enthusiast. The single track in Low Fields Road alongside Leeds United Football ground was, at one time, full from end to end whenever the first team was at home. Here we see about 30 (roughly half of the line), mainly 'Chamberlain' cars, awaiting the end of the game.

Crews could leave their trams and go to see the match without charge provided that they left the ground 10 minutes before the end of play (final score or not!) to get ready for the crowds that would be leaving shortly afterwards. Remember that these were the days when crowds regularly in excess of 40,000 were common with very little trouble, unlike today. Most people travelled to the ground by tram or bus, although a number of people living in south Leeds traditionally walked home.

On this particular day, 23 April 1955, Leeds were playing Blackburn Rovers and beat them 2-0, Brook scoring twice in front of a crowd of 39,208. It is interesting to relate that much of this trackwork can be seen to this day, having resurfaced above the tarmac. *A. K. Terry*

Below This is the same scene on 15 July 1991. The trams have long since departed, and the houses in the far distance are the only point of reference between the two views. *F. Whiley*

Above 'Horsfield' car No 191 approaches the top of Beeston Hill, passing a queue of people at the compulsory inward stop at Cemetery Road in June 1955. This was the place where each tram had to stop for the driver to put down the mechanical track brakes before proceeding carefully down the hill into town. Trams on this very busy route to Beeston last ran on 19 November 1955. *A. K. Terry*

Below All the property in the background of the previous view has long since disappeared – who would have thought that a city panorama lay behind the buildings at the top of Beeston Hill and Cemetery Road? This fascinating comparison shot, taken on 15 July 1991, reveals that only the pavement and fence on the left and the lamp-post to the left of the bus remain as reference points. *F. Whiley*

MEANWOOD
6
516
C.H. BEETHAM

11
GIPTON ESTATE
Parkinson's
For that EXTRA RISE
ALBATROSS
Self Raising
FLOUR
225

Left Here is a scene that would be totally unrecognisable today, the junction of Elland Road and Beeston Road at the 'Coach and Horses'. Motorway flyovers have now taken over, but on 23 June 1955, two days before the No 6 service was to finish, 'Feltham' No 516 rattles over the converging Beeston tracks on its way to Meanwood. A splendid 1.5-litre Riley completes the picture. *A. K. Terry*

Below left At Dewsbury Road terminus, during a quiet spell in May 1953, 'Horsfield' car No 225 is ready to move off downhill into the city on its way to Gipton. It is just before Coronation day, when many people would be cramming themselves into those few houses that were lucky enough to have 9, 12 or 14-inch televisions to witness the spectacle. It is inconceivable when one thinks of today's volume of traffic that this spot in the city could ever have been so quiet as portrayed here. *A. K. Terry*

Below In a particularly evocative 1950s suburban scene, in the late afternoon of 11 September 1954, typical brick terraced housing adjoins the 'Commercial Hotel' at the corner of Whingate and Wortley Road as 'Chamberlain' car No 147 gets under way on the long journey to Cross Gates.

A splendid example of the many thousands of gas lamps still lighting the streets at that time shows up well in the picture. The serried rows of chimneys (not a TV aerial in sight!) also stand out against a clear sky. How much better and more aesthetically pleasing the houses were when left as they were intended to be before the addition of the pathetic gas flues that have replaced so many chimney pots latterly. *A. K. Terry*

HALTON
20
554
DOCTOR IN THE HOUSE
Dougall's
GALLONS Ltd
ALF IBBOTSON
Bakers & Confectioners

14
CORN EXCHANGE
MELBOURNE ALES
93
KIRKSTALL ALES
HOTEL
THE FLEECE HOTEL
KIRKSTALL FINE ALES

Left 'Feltham' No 554 has just left New Inn on its way to Halton in this peaceful scene at Whingate junction on 16 June 1954. Employees from Roberts Signs are busy painting the hoardings, which feature a wonderful variety of adverts for Lifebuoy Soap, Johnson's Lavender Wax Polish, Player's Digger Flake and Guinness, which has used a popular film of the time, *Doctor in the House*, as promotion for its product by inserting 'and Guinness' after the word 'Doctor'.

The thousands of setts in the roadway are now a thing of the past; there can't be many people left who know how to lay them. Today there is absolutely nothing left to identify the scene. *A. K. Terry*

Below left At Stanningley, outside the 'Fleece Hotel' by Cohen's Foundry in April 1950, 'Chamberlain' car No 93, still in its pre-June 1948 blue and cream livery, is about to reverse and head back to the city. After the Pudsey route had been curtailed in 1938, only a few trams came to this point at peak times as an extension of the normal No 14 service to Half Mile Lane. *A. K. Terry*

Below Kirkstall Road near Willow Road traffic lights is the setting as 'Horsfield' car No 168 is about to go under the viaduct carrying the Leeds-Harrogate railway line. Service No 3 from Kirkstall to Harehills was abandoned on 3 April 1954, although the tracks were left in situ up to the Works until 7 November 1957.

Jubilee Stout – 'a head at all times' – was part of the Hope & Anchor Brewery in Sheffield in 1954. It subsequently became part of the Bass empire but can still be obtained today. *A. K. Terry*

In Headingley Lane, on the last day of tramway operation, 3 March 1956, the replacement bus stop can be seen, still covered up, on the left. Two 'Horsfield' cars, No 161 and the later to be preserved No 180, are about to pass just south of the old centre of Headingley by St Michael and All Angels Church, whose foundation stone was laid in 1884.

The 'tram pinch' road sign on the left indicated to motor vehicle drivers that the tracks were about to move closer to the kerbside. Woe betide any driver who did not treat the sign – and the tram – with respect. The latter would always win any argument! *A. K. Terry*

The tree on the left, with its fading white 'blackout' bands, is in full leaf and frames this scene in Otley Road perfectly. It is a quiet Sunday afternoon, 16 July 1955, as 'Chamberlain' car No 101 pauses on its way to Lawnswood.

The little girl with the tricycle and her parents take a breather as a West Yorkshire bus bound for Otley approaches the 'Three Horse Shoes'. This is an historic location as it was the terminus for the first horse-bus route in 1839. *A. K. Terry*

Here is a scene that has changed very little over the ensuing years, save for the vast increase in road traffic – Lawnswood terminus, on a cold afternoon in February 1956. 'Feltham' cars were rare visitors here and only really came during the last few weeks of the service. No 556 is about to reverse on the long journey to Roundhay.

At this time Lyons was 'blanket' advertising its 'Chico' coffee product – 'less than a 1d a cup'. The company seemed to have one of these extra adverts on at least one corner of every tram still running. *A. K. Terry*

It's a long time since the symbol for a school was the 'flame of learning'! Here we see one in Meanwood Road on 25 June 1955, and 'Horsfield' No 156 passing the end of Cambridge Road where, until 1934, trams turned left to go to Hyde Park via Woodhouse Street. This day in 1955 was significant – it was to be the last that trams would run along Meanwood Road.

A van belonging to George Dearlove, haulage contractor, is parked by period Wall's adverts for sausages and ice-cream. *A. K. Terry*

This is Meanwood Road at the junction of Bentley Lane. The last half-mile of the run to Meanwood was very pleasant, with part of Woodhouse Ridge, which was, and still is, a well-known and popular woodland recreation area, visible in the background.

Trams to Meanwood made their final journey on 25 June 1955, just four days after this picture was taken. Note the motor-cyclist wearing a crash helmet – long before they became compulsory. *A. K. Terry*

DEPOTS, WORKS AND INCIDENTS

The main Workshops at Kirkstall Road were always a place of great interest. Here, on 15 April 1956, the ex-London 'Feltham' car on the left is undergoing refurbishment before entering service, while 'Middleton Bogie' car No 267 is having a routine truck overhaul. The 'Feltham' on the right, still in its London livery and bearing the number 2128, has been stored for almost five years (its appearance certainly bears this out), and is destined never to enter service as Leeds No 572. Note its wartime headlamp mask still affixed.

Most internal tracks in the Works were connected by means of a traverser – basically a powered flat platform that ran in the foreground recess on its own rails. Trams could be run on to this platform and be moved around to wherever was necessary. A similar traverser can now be seen at the National Tramway Museum at Crich. The Works cat animates the otherwise peaceful scene. *A. K. Terry*

Another shot of the interior of Kirkstall Road Works, showing four cars awaiting attention on 17 April 1955. Ex-London 'Feltham' car No 2147 is awaiting refurbishment and eventual outshopping as Leeds No 587. *A. K. Terry*

A scene that many people would never know existed – track 23 of Swinegate Depot extended beyond the rear of the building, out into a yard and into one of the arches underneath Leeds City station. Here a number of trams would often be stored, some awaiting their final journey to the scrapyard. On this occasion, on 29 July 1955, one of the never-to-be-used 'Feltham' cars, ex-London United Tramways No 2145 (planned to be Leeds No 577) stands forlornly as ex-LNER 'B1' locomotive No 61306 shuffles past above. Unlike the tram, this engine was saved from the scrapyard and has been preserved with the name *Mayflower*. *A. K. Terry*

Another scene 'underneath the arches', a rare picture taken on 27 May 1956 of 'Chamberlain' car No 76, at the time used mainly on peak-hour duties. Several of these trams were stored here when not required for service. Within the arches the tracks split into two and, in later years, three. It was a desperate place, with rats and mice flourishing.

The tram tracks have long gone but the arch is still used as a private car park, now with a new pedestrian ramp into Neville Street. *A. K. Terry*

Chapeltown Depot closed for service trams on 23 April 1955, although it was used to store cars until August 1956. Here, in the early hours of 24 April 1955, 'Horsfield' No 162 prepares to leave the Depot as the final service car before returning to Swinegate.

Note the adverts on the wall to the left for the Civil Defence, which was still going strong at the time – the Cold War and the threat of nuclear attack were very much on people's minds. *A. K. Terry*

This shot of the interior of Chapeltown Depot was taken on 18 April 1955, just six days before closure. Note the cleaners' galleries alongside the top decks of the cars.

The building has since been substantially rebuilt, firstly for Leeds Corporation Supplies Dept and later for commercial purposes. *A. K. Terry*

Above No 197 was travelling on the 12 Circular through Middleton when it foundered in the appalling conditions of 25 February 1958, one of the rare occasions when a Leeds tram became well and truly stuck in the snow. It was photographed on the following day, when the sun was shining and the blizzard had abated. It remained abandoned for some time before works car No 6 finally got through from Belle Isle. *A. K. Terry*

Above right Works trams were often used to clear the winter snow. Here ex-Hull car No 6 (now preserved at Heaton Park, Manchester, in the form of Hull No 96), accompanied by works car No 2, stands just east of Halton terminus, having recently cleared the outbound track to Temple Newsam. They are waiting to cross over in order to clear the other track. It was common practice to leave the stretch between Halton and Temple Newsam to become one of the last snowbound sections when other more important routes needed clearing first. *A. K. Terry*

Right When it was thought that the worst of the winter was over, these 'snow broom' cars (there were five of them) were sometimes moved away from Swinegate. Here on 29 February 1956 we see No 5 turning into Chapeltown Depot to be stored until required the following winter. *A. K. Terry*

MAGNET PALE
6

CHAPELTOWN
2
544
5
5

2

WRIGHT'S BISCUITS
L.C.T.
1

Above left One of Leeds's last works trams was this former 'Chamberlain' car No 420, converted to open top and numbered 2, seen here standing in Torre Road Depot yard on 17 January 1956. A car like this was ideal for overhead inspection and wire replacement.

The tracks of this yard provided much of the pointwork used on the depot fan at the National Tramway Museum at Crich. *A. K. Terry*

Left Sheepscar junction is seen here from an unusual angle on 28 May 1954, with little works car No 1 towing a small trailer with American reciprocating rail-grinding equipment in it. It was a rather rare occasion to see the pair outside during the hours of daylight (they were normally nocturnal creatures) on their way to grind away some corrugations along Street Lane between Roundhay and Moortown.

Night pictures of the pair were almost impossible to take. They rarely stood still, although they appeared to do so when working; in fact, both tram and trailer moved along very slowly as the grinding proceeded, blurring any attempts at time-photography. The large box on the roof accommodates very heavy duty resistance equipment to permit the unit to move on the 'first notch' for a long period of time. *A. K. Terry*

Above A splendidly animated, posed shot at Parkside crossing on 26 June 1957 as a Hudswell Clarke 0-4-0 saddle tank waits for 'Feltham' car No 542 to pass on its way to Cross Gates. *A. K. Terry*

During the early evening of 31 May 1957 the roof cables of 'Feltham' No 504 caught fire. Sister car No 505 is endeavouring to push 504 over the busy Corn Exchange junction. The later part of this incident can be found on page 26, when 504 had been pushed on to the Call Lane loop to await eventual recovery and removal back to, presumably, Swinegate depot. *A. K. Terry*

Well-filled 'Chamberlain' car No 38 appears to have had an altercation with a motor-cyclist in Woodhouse Lane near the Fenton Hotel and outside Broadcasting House on 22 October 1955. Several tram crews appear to be offering assistance, although any injury does not seem to be severe. Any incidents like this put the trams in a bad light, of course, as hold-ups soon ensued. Today any such occurrence would have had the swift attention of the police and ambulance services, their vehicles screaming to the scene with an abundance of blue flashing lights.

The background shows the familiar outline of the Parkinson Building of the University complex. This was commenced before the last war, suspended during hostilities and finally completed in 1951, when it was opened by the Princess Royal. Notice the advert on the side of No 38 – the monocled gentleman in the bowler hat extolling the virtues of 'Sharps – the word for toffee'. This was a popular confection of the time that now seems to have disappeared. *A. K. Terry*

Not all tram casualties were accidental. It's 12.30am on 4 October 1957, service cars have returned to the depot, and it's time to despatch two 'Feltham' cars on their last ghostly journey to Low Fields Road scrapyard. Here we see No 562, which had been out of service for some considerable time, under her own power, literally dragging, by means of a length of chain, sister car No 539, which had suffered accident damage, out of Great Wilson Street into Meadow Lane. Both cars are at a virtual standstill, 562's wheels spinning furiously, motors whining with noise enough to wake the dead and sand being pumped on to the rails to try to gain adhesion; this can clearly be seen in the picture. The aftermath of all this activity can be vividly seen below... *A. K. Terry*

With unseemly haste the torch is put to No 562 in Low Fields Road scrapyard the following day, 5 October 1957. By this time any useful spares were no longer needed – only the metal body would be of any further use to anyone, and burning was the easiest and quickest way to reduce a tram to a twisted metal skeleton that could be carted off by the scrap-metal merchant. What a tragic end to a fine vehicle, which had first seen many years in London before transfer to Leeds in 1950. Car 539, which had been dragged by 562 to the yard, awaits its own fate behind.

The scrapyard was always the mess it looks in the picture, with bits of wood, tangled metal and broken glass scattered everywhere. The smoke and smell from the constant burning of cars must have been abominable – they'd never get away with it today! *A. K. Terry*

Left A sad sight – three 'Felthams' that never made it into service, seen here on 10 November 1956 in Low Fields Road scrapyard. Several of these cars were fitted with bow collectors and connected up to make them runable so that they could be moved into storage, usually in Torre Road Depot yard.

The front car shown here, London Transport No 2135, should have become Leeds No 584 – its number has been chalked on the front. The burned-out remains of another unused 'Feltham' lie alongside. *A. K. Terry*

Below left A sight that was becoming all too common as each tram service finished: this is Lawnswood on the night of 3 March 1956. 'Horsfield' No 222 had been the last car from City Square on service No 1 and was besieged by souvenir-hunting students. As a result the tram was damaged and did not return to service for several days. *A. K. Terry*

Above right In 1949 one of the last new sections of route in Britain was that built to join up Middleton with Belle Isle along the Middleton Ring Road. In this picture most of the rails have been laid and traction poles erected, but the overhead wiring is still to be installed. This section was opened as a Circular service – No 12 via Middleton and No 26 via Belle Isle – on 28 August 1949. *A. K. Terry*

Right However, four years later here is Stanningley Road on 18 October 1953, shortly after the withdrawal of service No 14 to Half Mile Lane. Certain works trams had passed along the reserved tracks as far as Bramley in the weeks following closure in order to 'scrub' the rails (ie to clean away some of the corrugations) ready for re-use elsewhere. The wires and remaining track were, however, soon taken down and covered up.

This scene, taken on a Sunday morning, shows men at work dropping the running wires near the 'Daisy Inn' – still going strong today. This would become an all too familiar scene over the ensuing six years. *A. K. Terry*

DAISY INN
TETLEY'S
PLAYERS NAVY CUT
NEWTON
FOR

PRESERVED CARS

The confines of Kirkstall Road Works on 15 April 1956. 'Beeston Air Brake' car No 399, one of the last of its type to be withdrawn, was used for many years thereafter as a shunter in the Works. Note that all the vestibule windows were sans glass so that drivers could see what they were doing rather than have to clean it. The extra high steelwork on the fender helped in moving odd cars around, some of which were mounted high on special Works trucks.

Having thus survived until the tramway system closed in 1959, No 399 was donated to the then budding Tramway Museum Society. It arrived at Crich, the museum's home in Derbyshire, as the Society's second car and stood for some time near the present entrance. The full restoration of this car to its former glory in a chocolate and primrose livery was only completed in 1990 and the car is now running as one of the main operational fleet at the museum.

Cephos will bring back memories to older readers as being a popular headache remedy of earlier times. *A. K. Terry*

'Convert' car No 345 survived after withdrawal in 1948 by becoming a joiners' store in Swinegate Depot, here seen on 18 November 1957. It was one of 34 similar trams, all rebuilt from former open-balcony cars between 1935 and 1942, 12 of which remained without air-brakes. Here the car has been moved to the back of the Depot out of use, but earmarked for possible preservation. By chance, 'Horsfield' car No 180, which was also subsequently selected for preservation, is standing at one side just before entering peak-hour service.

Car No 345 has remained in store for more than 40 years at Crich. She is now the subject of a major rebuild and will take to the rails again splendidly refurbished in a year or so.

The 'Converts', as older people of Leeds will remember, were many folks' favourites at a time when most other trams had only restricted upper-deck forward vision because of the large destination and route number indicators. *A. K. Terry*

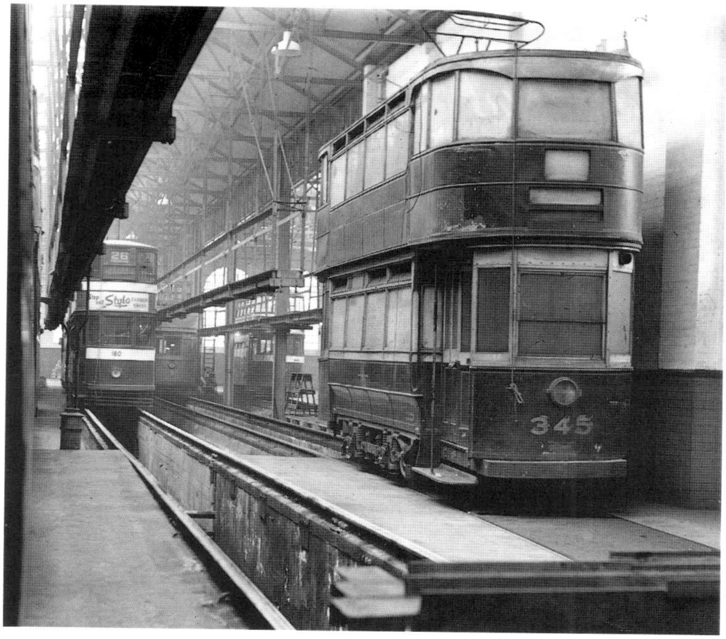

It is a fine, sunny early Sunday morning, 29 September 1957, at Moortown corner, and the previous evening had seen the last trams run along Chapeltown Road to Moortown; however, trams continued to run here via Roundhay, although from this date only to and from Briggate via Harehills, as service No 9 to Dewsbury Road had also been abandoned.

'Horsfield' car No 180 is the first car of the day to work this 'new' No 3 service, and became the one subsequently preserved and completely renovated at the National Tramway Museum at Crich.

Note the road sign on the extreme right of the picture – in 1957 an everyday object taken for granted, but now a thing very much of the past. *A. K. Terry*

Left In the early part of the last war there was a shortage of trams in Leeds, so during 1942 a total of 32 cars were bought from Hull Corporation for further use within the city; several more were purchased in 1945. Unpopular with passengers, they were nicknamed 'Kipper Boxes' but were sturdy, reliable trams. They were all withdrawn by 1951, the last survivor, coincidentally also having been the first to enter service, being No 446.

Fortunately 446 was put into store for preservation. On 2 June 1955 it was finally loaded on to a Pickfords road trailer and taken away to an outdoor site near Bury. Today the car is part of the National Tramway Museum collection, but having been restored eventually in Hull as No 132, it is now on display as part of that city's transport collection. *A. K. Terry*

Below 'Feltham' No 501 was the first former London car of its type to arrive in Leeds in September 1949, having come on loan with a possible view to buying further cars of the class. As it transpired, it was considered so successful that the whole 92 were purchased, although as previously mentioned only 90 actually came to the city, and of those 90 only 83 were to enter service. No 501 ran for some time in London Transport livery as No 2099, but was subsequently renumbered, with the remainder numbered in sequence as they arrived. Here, on 27 May 1958, No 501 is seen 'out in the wilds' approaching Temple Newsam terminus. As can clearly be seen, something has given the dash end a fair old clout. Whether the 'Felthams' were as successful as was first envisaged is doubtful. Many crews, particularly drivers, hated them – they were notoriously temperamental at stopping. Nevertheless, they served the city well for the comparatively short time they were in Leeds, and No 501 was saved from the scrapyard. She now resides in the London Transport Museum, Covent Garden, repainted in her original Metropolitan Electric Tramway livery. *A. K. Terry*

Right The other 'Feltham' car to be preserved is No 526, seen here at the 'Irwin Arms Hotel' at Halton in August 1958. She subsequently went on her longest ever single journey to the USA, where she found a new home at the Seashore Trolley Museum, Kennebunkport, Maine. Unfortunately she has languished since with no sign of ever running again. What a great achievement and thrill it would be to have her returned home and put into working order. *A. K. Terry*

Below London County Council's experimental tram No 1 came to Leeds in 1951 and ran as No 301 for around six years. It is seen here on 26 November 1957 standing outside the coal yard in South Accommodation Road after being loaded to travel back to London for initial exhibition with the London Transport Collection at Clapham. Later the car was moved to the National Tramway Museum where, after a cosmetic repaint, it now stands in London Transport Executive red and cream as No 1 again. *A. K. Terry*

SAXA
Player's Please
SHELL
ICA
COX & Co
WEST YORKSHIRE FOUNDRIES LTD.
DEPOT
OVALTINE

OPEL
WASS
AUTO SMART
M

Above left On 4 August 1954 the tram approaching along Hunslet Road is 'brand new' single-decker No 600. This car originally arrived in Leeds from Sunderland in 1944 in a much different form from that shown here. It then underwent a 10-year period of storage and spasmodic attempts to convert it in accordance with various ideas of the day. This was its first time in public service, although it only ran for three short years until September 1957, operating exclusively on the No 25 service between Swinegate and Hunslet; it never worked even one fare-paying passenger-carrying journey on any other service. It is now preserved at the National Tramway Museum.

Of the three companies mentioned on the wall of Chadwick Street on the left, only George Depledge survives to this day. *A. K. Terry*

Left The tram may have been preserved, but here is the same scene on 15 July 1991. The wall of the building on the right is all that remains at the junction of Chadwick Street and Hunslet Road. *F. Whiley*

Above The two railcars, Nos 601 and 602, could fill a chapter of the book all on their own; they were truly magnificent vehicles and looked regal in their special livery of royal purple, cream and gold leaf lining. In their early life in 1953 and 1954 they visited many parts of the city on various routes, but finally settled down to work the No 25 from Swinegate to Hunslet. Both survived until the end of the system and both were subsequently preserved. No 601 was purchased by the Middleton Railway Preservation Society and 602, seen here on 17 June 1954 at Whingate terminus, went to Crich, where it is in working order. Unfortunately, No 601 met an untimely fate at the hands of vandals and was subsequently burned out in 1963. *A. K. Terry*

INDEX OF LOCATIONS